NO-NONSENSE INNOVATION

PRACTICAL STRATEGIES *for* SUCCESS

T0106747

BILL LOWE

with CARY SHERBURNE

MORGAN JAMES PUBLISHING • NEW YORK

NO-NONSENSE INNOVATION

ISBN: 978-1-60037-489-0 (Paperback)
ISBN: 978-1-60037-490-6 (Hardcover)

Library of Congress Control Number: 2008936948

Published by:

www.morganjamespublishing.com

Morgan James Publishing, LLC
1225 Franklin Ave Suite 325
Garden City, NY 11530-1693
Toll Free 800-485-4943
www.MorganJamesPublishing.com

Cover/Interior Design by:
Rachel Lopez
rachel@r2cdesign.com

To Frank Carey, who had the courage to defy conventional wisdom, and

without whose leadership, the IBM PC would never have been possible.

And to my wife, Cristina, for her love, energy, support and patience.

I also dedicate this book to my children, Gabriela, Danny, Jim, Julie

and Michele, and the wonderful grandchildren whose lives I hope will be

positively impacted by all of the innovations that are in store

for them in the road ahead.

"Never doubt that a small group of committed people can change the world. Indeed, it is the only thing that ever has."

MARGARET MEAD (1901-1978)
AMERICAN ANTHROPOLOGIST

ACKNOWLEDGEMENT

I have been blessed with significant support in developing the Pragmatic Innovation process and putting the material together for this book.

Dating back to my time at Xerox Corporation, the work process represented here has benefited greatly from my wife, Cristina's, contributions. As a wife, friend, and a terrific partner, she has provided a great deal of insight based on years of sales and marketing experience. We have grown together from our joint experiences in over thirty companies and we have developed a greater clarity in the innovation process. Without her constant support, encouragement and commitment to the integrity of this effort by challenging and testing my theories and work, I could not have found the way to articulate the direction of much of this work. As a devoted mom, most of all, I appreciate her willingness to do this while managing her career and raising two fantastic children, Cristina Gabriela and William Daniel.

As the work on this book progressed, Shane Greenstein of Northwestern University was particularly helpful and encouraging. He supported the work, and he introduced me to a number of people who would later be of great assistance in this journey. His students are very lucky to have such a knowledgeable, enthusiastic, and passionate mentor. As the book took shape, Jim Cordata of IBM was also extremely helpful and full of good suggestions regarding its development.

I learned from Frank Carey at IBM, David Kearns at Xerox Corporation, and many current entrepreneurs who are always there to help me witness the principles of innovation in process. Important leaders and innovators that have shaped the projects discussed in this book include Lou Eggebrech at IBM, Chip Holt at Xerox Corporation, Charlie Coppi at Gulfstream, Denise Miano at NEPS, and recently, Jim Hare and Chuck Hale at QWK2LRN.

In my many years in both corporate and entrepreneurial life, I have had the pleasure of knowing many other people whose great ideas, supportive leadership, commitment to competitive awareness, and industry knowledge have brought some element of innovation into their workplace, and I take a moment to applaud these individuals who know I have valued their efforts.

To write a book of this nature, I needed a special partner to assist in the project day to day. Cary Sherburne approached me with the idea of writing this book and has been resourceful, encouraging, and diligent as we worked together on the project. I have thoroughly enjoyed this collaborative effort to launch what I believe is an important strategy that can bring value to future innovators at a time when the need for change, innovation, and vision has never been greater.

TABLE OF CONTENTS

FOREWORD

Puzzle and Treasure

By Shane Greenstein

All students of the computer industry have heard of Bill Lowe, the leader of an IBM Boca Raton facility that launched the IBM PC. That launch was a signal event in computing. It catalyzed growth in the small systems market.

For students of the computer industry, IBM's decisions always seemed somewhat puzzling. The PC was the first open design in IBM's history. While it worked out well for IBM for a number of years, nothing in IBM history pointed to such a change in strategic direction at that time. Crucial facts had to be missing from common accounts.

It takes an insider to explain the puzzles of the past.

I have had the pleasure of sitting down with Bill Lowe on several occasions to discuss his managerial philosophy. In personal conversation, Lowe has the same voice that is reflected in the text of this book by Lowe and Sherburne. The voice is honest, calm, and down to earth, as well as precise, respectful, and authoritative.

In brief, Bill Lowe possesses a gift. He can speak truth to power, even when he is opposing the not-invented-here syndrome that is all too common in many companies. Lowe was both the right messenger and manager to change company policy. It is no wonder Frank Carey invited Lowe to speak to the management committee in the summer of 1980, even though he was relatively junior in the company at the time.

Do not misinterpret me. I came to Bill Lowe looking to solve an old puzzle, but I walked away with much more from my reading of Lowe and Sherburne.

As a student of the impact of innovation on business success, I found a great deal of wisdom in Lowe's no-nonsense approach to managing open innovation. This book has found a sublime solution to a problem that has become more vexing as innovation has become more complex. Namely, it explains a mechanism that allows a mainstream organization to not remain static.

The blend of fascinating autobiographical stories with guidance for business people at all levels makes for a fascinating read. Bill Lowe's easy-to-follow, hands-on, pragmatic approach is a process that can be leveraged by organizations of all types and sizes.

This entire book is a treasure.

INTRODUCTION

*"Every organization needs one core competence: Innovation.
And every organization needs a way to record
and appraise its innovative performance."*

PETER DRUCKER

Over my career with Fortune 500 companies and small technology startups, my greatest satisfaction has been derived from creating new and profitable products and businesses. I have been fortunate to have a wide range of rich opportunities that have allowed me to exercise my passion for innovation. Through my years of experience with introducing innovation to a number of different organizations in varying industries and disciplines, I have developed a model or methodology that I believe any executive can translate into excellence in innovation within his or her own business. In this book, I will be sharing my experiences with a few unique and personal opportunities in American business that generated breakthrough new business and products for major companies, resulting in the development of brand-new multi-billion-dollar businesses in several cases. The underlying experience-based and strategic model that enabled these successes and which is the primary subject of this book is a no-nonsense approach to innovation that can be easily employed by managers and business owners across a wide spectrum of industries and disciplines. We term this process **Pragmatic Innovation.** It is a practical, proven and replicable approach to establishing and maintaining a culture of innovation within any organization, large or small. Throughout the rest of the book, we will use the terms "No-Nonsense Innovation" and "Pragmatic Innovation" interchangeably.

One of the hottest research and development principles today is the theme of Open Innovation. Our no-nonsense Pragmatic Innovation process is built on a foundation of Open Innovation, but Pragmatic Innovation takes the typically technology-oriented practice a major step further. Open Innovation is described by Henry Chesbrough in his definitive work, *Open Innovation: The New Imperative for Creating and Profiting from Technology[1]*, and his follow-on book, *Open Business Models: How to Thrive in the New Innovation Landscape.[2]* Chesbrough describes a process of innovation that allows ideas to flow out of the company in order to find better sites for monetization and to flow into the company as new offerings and new business models. He contrasts this to the conventional method of conducting business, where intellectual property is primarily developed in-house, and guarded jealously whether or not it is ever monetized. Chesbrough's work focuses primarily on the research and development aspects of the business and the cultural barriers

---

1   Open Innovation, by Henry Chesbrough, Harvard Business School Press, 2003
2   Open Business Models, by Henry Chesbrough, Harvard Business School Press, 2006

to innovation that many companies erect, knowingly or unknowingly, as they strive to protect what they consider to be their crown jewels—their intellectual property.

In *Open Business Models,* Chesbrough expands the concept somewhat to service businesses that have been affected by Open Innovation concepts, notably Hollywood studios and the mortgage industry. In those two examples, business models were dramatically changed due to the development of intermediate markets. In the studio example, the older model where the studio "owned" everything, including the actors, has migrated into a collaborative process that involves a multitude of parties, each bringing a different area of specialization to the process. Chesbrough refers to this as an "ecosystem of innovation" that has resulted in the old studio system vanishing, replaced by a collage of independent (from each other) players ranging from actors and screenwriters to agents, special effects specialists, directors, and producers.

The mortgage example discusses a migration away from the local bank as the nearly exclusive source of home mortgages, to today's world where mortgages are often originated by one entity, serviced by another entity, and may be traded to numerous different holders over their life. Anyone who has recently acquired a mortgage has probably experienced this model.

Aside from these two services examples, which do not involve intellectual property (IP) as part of the innovation process, the majority of the theory revolves around how companies develop, buy, sell, and manage IP from internal and external sources, and how they establish business models that can take advantage of internal or external IP to generate new revenue streams. Chesbrough also points out that most companies underutilize their IP, leaving— in many cases—as much as 90 percent of it unused and "on the shelf."

Pragmatic Innovation takes IP and the R&D environment into consideration, establishing a framework for ensuring optimum utilization of both internal and external IP. But beyond that, it is a broader, business-based philosophy that starts with the C-suite—the CEO and his or her staff—and the manner in which that team manages the business and inspires people to stay fresh, innovative and energized. Throughout my career, I have intuitively applied this philosophy with very successful results. And I now believe I have been able to distill it down to a repeatable process that has value for almost any business.

In fact, over the last several years, beyond the seminal stories I will share with you in this book, I have met with more than 30 executive management teams within both large corporations and small start-ups to help them develop winning innovative strategies. These recent successes, along with those earlier in my career, have convinced me that success in innovating requires leadership with a disciplined yet fresh view. It also requires leadership that is willing to reach outside the comfort zone and is open to doing things differently, coupled with a desire to continuously keep the organization moving and alive.

Peter Drucker, one of the world's foremost management thinkers and writers, perhaps said it best when he noted:

> *The Innovative Organization understands that innovation starts with an idea. Ideas are somewhat like babies—they are born small, immature and shapeless. In the Innovative organization, executives do not say, "This is a damn-fool idea." Instead they say, "What would be needed to make this embryonic, half baked, foolish idea into something that makes sense, that is feasible, that is an opportunity for us?"*[3]

---

3   The Daily Drucker: 366 Days of Insight and Motivation for Getting the Right Things Done, by Peter F. Drucker, Collins, October 2004

In this book, I have incorporated stories of how some "half baked ideas," such as the original concept for the IBM personal computer, were translated into extreme business success by applying the no-nonsense principles of Pragmatic Innovation. The process is a realistic, feasible, practical, and replicable approach in that it can operate within the dynamics of any company's culture and organizational structure.

Based on my years of experience applying Pragmatic Innovation, the process can be distilled into ten critical and essential components. The rules are flexible enough to work for companies ranging from a million dollar start-up to a billion dollar Fortune 500 company, yet offer a structure that allows organizations to drive innovation. This process is proven, and for many companies, has driven improved revenues in new markets, increased market share in existing markets, and new products and new strategic initiatives that are vital to continued organizational growth.

As CEO of several companies, and the visionary leader tasked with driving new innovation, I have also had the opportunity to interact with many well-known people and corporations at a very personal level. I am a believer that stories are an important part of communicating strategic concepts such as Pragmatic Innovation, and so I have also woven some of my anecdotal experiences into this book to demonstrate Pragmatic Innovation on a personal and human level. I hope the reader can draw some parallels from these stories to his or her own company and life. From CEOs to top entertainers, scientists, celebrities, and others with whom I have had the good fortune and opportunity to work and to get to know on a personal level, I have gained great insight into the workings of American business. These experiences have also taught me how Pragmatic Innovation can be applied to make business more exciting. I believe that a spirit of innovation and a willingness to do "big and different" things is what drives extraordinary achievement. I hope this passion will resonate throughout the book and that from it you will gain knowledge and a process that you can apply in your own world.

Each chapter is structured around corporate experiences I have had that demonstrate the impact of Pragmatic Innovation, except for the last chapter. This chapter focuses on an exciting public sector project with a goal of revolutionizing primary and secondary education worldwide through the principles of Pragmatic Innovation.

The book lays out a specific process that others can take advantage of, leveraging my experience. Toward that end, there are ten key success factors for Pragmatic Innovation that will be explored in depth through the rest of this book.

> 1. *The initial idea or strategy has to be embraced by an executive team that is willing to believe in the value of innovation within the organization.*
>
> Large organizations often have a strong tendency to stick with the *status quo,* or at a minimum, depend on what they believe are trusted, tried-and-true behaviors that have delivered success in the past. The executive team must be proactive in supporting—and even demanding—new ideas and new thinking that are often contrary to the historical past. It is absolutely critical to break through corporate paradigms that can keep these ideas buried or hidden and prevent fresh thinking.
>
> One major project I conducted in Arizona at the request of the then-President of the University of Arizona was designed to obtain increased value from the research activity underway at the University. We defined why the University of Arizona's process was not working. We then deployed a new and exciting

process to address the issues we had uncovered. As a result, the University established a Technology Transfer office and developed community entrepreneurial support programs. Our role as innovators was to question the *status quo* and to understand how their process was broken. Part of that learning was to find out how other universities achieved success in this area.

In small entrepreneurial organizations with a natural tendency to innovate, it can be difficult for the founder to be comfortable with ideas not of his or her invention. Small organizations are often dominated by a founder who is concerned about losing control. We have many examples that demonstrate how the Pragmatic Innovation process has been used to help these organizations move forward.

2. *At the highest level possible, but always at the C-level, there should be an executive sponsor who is willing to take risks and has the courage to fight the antipathy to change that most organizations experience.*

Companies often have silos and internal political orientations that make it difficult to embrace change. Many times they are excessively selective about who is authorized to initiate change and innovation. The executive sponsor must be willing to "break glass" and encourage team(s) to continuously improve their performance, taking an outside view of what can potentially be done to continue to innovate. There is no question that the higher the level in the organization at which the executive sponsor resides, the easier it is to drive Pragmatic Innovation throughout the organization. As you will see in Chapter Two, then Chairman and CEO of IBM Frank Carey was just such an example of an executive sponsor who did an outstanding job of fostering innovation. But this Pragmatic Innovation mindset should not be limited to the hallowed halls of the C-Suite. It must permeate the organization at all levels in an open environment that allows those with less seniority to present their ideas to top tier management with an expectation that they will at least be considered.

In some companies, as I will describe later, too many senior executives "drink from their own bathwater." This is often because of the lack of new talent at that level. Mixing the best of your inside talent with people from outside the organization who have succeeded with different approaches is essential. Recently, a very talented friend of mine has assumed a high-level marketing position with a $3 billion bottling company. I know that his new ideas and fresh approach will engender innovation and thought-provoking discussion, simply because he is not part of the established culture.

3. *The leader who is the emissary or agent of change must be someone who is willing to think openly and drive innovation.*

Change agents and innovators can arise from anywhere in the organization, but true no-nonsense Pragmatic Innovation occurs only when their passion and commitment is allowed to drive fresh new ideas throughout the organization. Executive emissaries of change must work hard to ensure that innovation is allowed to thrive and survive.

As we were developing the IBM PC, there were crucial moments that required IBM senior leadership to actively foster the progress of the initiative, protecting it from others in the organization who had a vested interest in maintaining the *status quo*. Often organizations have a stop-and-go approach to new ideas, either because project leaders give these projects a half-hearted effort or are reassigned at a critical juncture within the project to another job within the organization. Personal insecurities, especially in the face of strong organizational resistance, all too often make it easier to play it safe than to break glass to get the job done.

4. *The project team must be able to work outside of its historical comfort zone and should be cross-functional, operational in nature, and in touch with the external customer base.*

With good leadership, a willing team with proven operational experience can carry an innovative project to the next level. The more operationally diverse the team is, the greater its credibility and effectiveness in bringing the new product or idea to fruition. Many times organizations will simply assign a sales or development group to the innovation team rather than deploying a true cross-functional team. This can doom the project before it even starts, since it will be very difficult to obtain organizational buy-in.

5. *An honest, data driven assessment of internal strengths and weaknesses must be conducted without the constraints of historical beliefs and biases, even those that have delivered success in the past.*

With strong use of the principles of total quality management, Six Sigma, and other quality-based systems that rely on good internal and external data, innovation will have a greater chance of success. Many organizations make decisions based upon "gut feel" relative to the impact that innovation will have externally. Using a more pragmatic and disciplined approach is more likely to ensure success. Constantly testing and evaluating shifts and changes in the marketplace in a timely, data-driven manner ensures that new directions will supply marketable value at their completion.

6. *The organization must conduct an external benchmarking effort involving customers, competitors, suppliers, distributors and other business partners to discover alternative opportunities and innovative trends in the industry.*

Although external benchmarking, in principle, is an easy concept to understand, it is an area of pitfall for many companies. As extensive as IBM resources were at the time of the PC launch, there was a lack of true organizational understanding about nontraditional competitors that were nipping at IBM's heels. In the year prior to embarking on the initiative to launch the PC, our skunk works group came to understand how different our approach needed to be given the information we had discerned from our external analysis of suppliers and other technology companies. Most importantly, we foresaw the impact of the manner in which the emerging breed of software developers was implementing new strategies to build and write independent software offerings. We believed these dynamics required a drastic change in business process if the IBM PC was going to be a success.

In another example, I was recently working with a manufacturing company that services one of the Big Four automotive companies. During this work, it became clear that state-of-the-art practices in the automotive parts and supply industry were no longer geographically based in the United States, given the shifts and changes in the global marketplace. This perspective helped the team understand that a global view of best practices and operational excellence was critical to driving manufacturing innovation.

7. *The innovation team needs to develop a strategy and an architecture that exploits the top opportunities that have been identified.*

In the more than 30 companies I have worked with to drive Pragmatic Innovation into the culture, an architected view of the landscape always emerged. As you will see from the materials we developed to convince the IBM Corporate Management Committee to proceed with development of the IBM PC, an architecture was structured to define innovative thought in both technology and in the application of business terms and conditions.

In a small technology company with whom I am currently working, we have architected a view of the marketplace it serves. This will allow us to address the critical components where we can and must contribute. It also helps us understand where our best market fit lies. To try to reduce this knowledge to one page can be difficult. Few companies take the time to so crisply define not only who they are, and what their expertise and focus are, but how their innovation fits from an architected standpoint. From this simple one- to two-page template, which I will share with you in this book, can emerge the next level of architecture that defines what a company needs to do to ensure its future. What we understood at IBM as we architected the new PC product was that the business approach used in the IBM mainframe corporate world would not be effective in bringing the PC to market, and standing still was not an option. Steve Jobs' innovation with the iPOD is a classic example of the pre-music Apple computer hardware company architecting a completely restructured view of products and services to support the music demands of its new customer base.

8. *Leadership and the innovation team must work to create consensus around the defined strategic direction while recognizing the need to overcome organizational inertia—both with people and with processes.*

When new projects are underway, it is important that the stakeholders be informed about—and thoroughly understand—the merits of the project. In a small organization, this is quite easy and is usually accomplished through informal communications. But in larger organizations, it becomes problematic. A communications balance must be reached, weighing the ongoing concern of confidentiality prior to any product launch against the need to know. However, innovation developed in an organizational vacuum and tossed over the transom rarely succeeds. Selecting a cross-functional innovation team from the outset can assist in this critical communications process.

9. *A Pragmatic Innovation Implementation Plan© will include ongoing benchmarking and strategic refreshment, recognizing the tendency of the organization to fight change over time and to revert to "business as usual."*

Simply look at government agencies, which are bloated with people but have lost any innovative perspective to enable them to grasp the importance of this principle. I spent a few years in the aviation industry and have made more than one trip to the FAA. In many ways, the agency has remained immune to innovation. Today's consumers buy simple, relatively inexpensive GPS systems, carried in their cars or on their persons, that can direct them anywhere at any time. The Gulfstream jets ten years ago carried them as well, yet these devices are not an industry standard in the commercial airline industry. Without ongoing benchmarking and strategic refreshment orchestrated from the top, organizations large and small, public and private, are more likely to remain satisfied with the *status quo* and thus discourage innovation.

I am a strong believer that the spirit of innovation is one of the most fundamental mechanisms enabling businesses, individuals, and society to be able to sustain an improved quality of life. When the U.S. rallied to President Kennedy's challenge to be the first country to send a man to the moon, we drove amazing new innovation that affected technologies across the spectrum of materials, aerodynamics and aviation; human survival; and a litany of new products. The Internet and all of its associated innovation has impacted how we bank, how we learn, how we share information, and how we collaborate globally. Yet the Internet is only in its infancy.

"Plus la change, plus la meme chose." The more things change, the more they remain the same—despite claims otherwise. Companies must structure themselves to embrace change in order to avoid this most fatal of pitfalls in the innovation process.

10. *A culture of continuous improvement with clear measurement processes must be established to continually drive innovation into the future.*

I call this the "higher road." As soon as you have started to drive along the coastline and want to move higher up the mountain, you have to find the next "higher road." So many organizations have launched one or two successful products only to find themselves mired back in a non-innovative state again. Unfortunately, this is what happened with IBM and the PC. The company lost the potential to take the next step to drive greater market share and new values. Xerox Corporation had a history of developing significant innovation in its Palo Alto Research Center (PARC). But it also had a history of allowing those innovations to be usurped by competitors, as we will discuss in Chapter Three.

Pragmatic Innovation is not a theoretical exercise. There is a structured, easy-to-follow process that has been used and tested successfully in many businesses on many occasions. It includes development, marketing, requirements definition, business development, and a strong focus on customers and competitors. My objective in this book is to equip you to employ the principles of Pragmatic Innovation in your own business. Through this process, I believe you and your company can benefit from establishing a culture of innovation within the organization.

In the Beginning

The concept for this book began when Cary Sherburne, my co-author, approached me in 2006 with an idea for a book that would tell the IBM PC story from my vantage point inside the organization. I have often been referred to as the Father of the IBM PC. With respect to the history of how the IBM PC came to market, the story has been told from many different perspectives. The difference between this writing and other accounts lies in the detailed aspects of the development of the IBM PC that have never before been shared publicly. This inside-IBM view and perspective is presented in Chapter Two.

As we began to embark on this project, I also discussed with Cary a number of the rich experiences I had subsequent to IBM and the many intriguing people I came in contact with during those years. It was amazing to work with brilliant people such as Bill Gates and Steve Jobs; to meet Warren Buffet; to travel with Mohammed Al Fayad; to share dinners and experiences with the likes of Bill Cosby, Paul Orfalea, Steve Forbes, and so many others. As we talked through all of the elements, the project got bigger. It was clear that beyond the interesting—and sometimes startling—inside stories from IBM and other companies where I held executive positions, there was a valuable business philosophy that was also worth communicating. We decided to write this book to:

- Provide new historical insight into the birth of the IBM PC;

- Provide the necessary tools and principles for Pragmatic Innovation by coupling real-world examples with definitive how-to steps that can benefit any executive;

- And finally, to have some fun along the way, sharing stories about some of the most memorable personalities that I have encountered during my fifty-plus years in a very exciting, diverse, educational, and unusual career.

The process of Pragmatic Innovation is relatively simple, but in this book, it is packaged in a way that provides actionable advice to executives on how to shift their innovation model to better meet the demands of today's dynamic marketplace. It recognizes the importance of leveraging the value of their intellectual property and internal knowledge base while at the same time benefiting from external resources, perspectives, and ideas. This is exactly what occurred with the IBM PC, and it was repeated again with similar success with the Xerox DocuTech and the Gulfstream GV. I have also worked in older industries, with companies smaller in size and less advanced in their technologies such as Moore Corporation and New England Business Services. Application of the principles of Pragmatic Innovation made extremely positive contributions to these organizations as well, and there is much to learn from sharing our experiences there.

The business landscape is littered with companies that have forgotten how to innovate—or never knew how in the first place. Understanding some of those failures is important as well. To that end, I also discuss what does *not* work. Within any organization, there are natural forces that work against innovation, especially in established companies. There are always individuals at multiple levels in the organization—particularly at the top—that are threatened by change. They often work hard to protect what they perceive as their established territory. There are also internal cultural paradigms that have become so entrenched that companies almost do not realize they are there—and that they are harmful and unyielding to change. Many companies and individuals remain satisfied with the *status quo*, even in the face of compelling evidence that the *status quo* will only lead to a declining business. Even small companies that have tremendous potential and many new ideas are often constrained by the disease I term "Founder's Fever"; that is, the tendency of founders to try to control everything instead of supporting change and the development of more mature processes, sharing responsibility with others in order to more effectively grow and scale the organization. Being forewarned about these pitfalls is being forearmed to avoid them.

We truly believe that by following the Pragmatic Innovation process, any company can protect and nurture its innovators; attract new innovation; and benefit from the energy, creativity, and market leadership inherent in a truly innovative organization. You will see that throughout this book.

Pragmatic Innovation in Practice

Few people know the true inside story of the IBM PC. Few people realize how difficult it was to propose such an innovative idea given the historical period and the cultural dynamics within this traditional, mainframe-driven and conservative company. Nor do many people consider the legal oversight under which IBM was operating during this period. Finally, few people have ever seen the actual documentation that was presented to the IBM Corporate Management Committee as this project was being developed. All of this is included in Chapter Two.

Most narratives of the IBM PC story would have you believe that IBM put the personal computer together in a matter of weeks. That simply is not true. I will share a more accurate view that details the type of studies, consultations, and review of trends that were behind key decisions that determined how the IBM PC would be positioned. Those elements are also included in Chapter Two.

Although I did not think about it this way at the time, the deployment of the IBM PC was my first experience utilizing the principles of Pragmatic Innovation. In hindsight, I recognize that I could not have succeeded in this landmark project without the courage and support of Frank Carey, the then Chairman and CEO of IBM, as you will see. Before the age of forty, I had the opportunity of a lifetime and the risk of a lifetime, rolled into one not-always-so-tidy package—to be an agent of change in a phenomenal period of technological history, and to create one of the most exciting products that any corporation has ever launched. The legacy of the IBM PC affects almost every facet of life today. It has been a major factor in changing the way information is deployed, used, and communicated by businesses, educational institutions and individuals worldwide.

An important meeting that took place three years prior to the launch of the PC would be a harbinger of the future for me. In 1977, I had the pleasure of meeting Ted Nelson. I was so impressed with him that I invited him to speak at an IBM executive team meeting where I was hoping to garner support for the development of microcomputer-based products within the company. This meeting was ultimately held in Atlanta in 1978.

First, a little background on Ted Nelson:

> Theodor (Ted) Holm Nelson[4] was Actor Celeste Holm's son from her marriage to director Ralph Nelson. He is an American sociologist, philosopher, and pioneer of information technology. Ted coined the term "hypertext" in 1963, and he first published it in 1965. He is also credited with first use of the words hypermedia and virtuality, among others. The main thrust of his work has

---

4 Biographical information obtained from Wikipedia (www.wikipedia.org) and other Web sources, April 2007.

been to acknowledge that computers should be easily accessible to ordinary people. He has been quoted as saying:

A user interface should be so simple that a beginner in an emergency can understand it within ten seconds.

When I engaged Ted Nelson to speak at this IBM management group meeting, he was a young guy, and he didn't wear a tie—this was almost anathema to the buttoned-up IBM managers who were attending this meeting. He had put a two-hour presentation together for this dinner meeting. I have to say, it was very amateurish compared to what we were used to, but the message was powerful. He had created images which he projected onto the wall with a slide projector. They showed him accessing information from the middle of the jungle, on a sandy beach, and from other remote locations. He called this process "XANADU." His whole message that evening was that communication and computer technology was moving in the direction of "*making all information available to all people, no matter who they were, or when, where and how they wanted it.*" This is a concept that seems fairly simplistic in today's world of wireless communications and the Web, with Blackberrys and iPhones everywhere. But thirty years ago, it was revolutionary thinking. Not only was I intrigued with this message and with the vision of where it could take us, but it was a defining moment for me. It helped shape a new perspective about a new information age, and I began to be able to communicate its power to those at IBM who had remained thus far unconvinced and resistant to change.

Based in part on this early, innovative vision from Ted Nelson, together with my subsequent experiences in launching new technology, I have become a firm believer that the best way to judge the viability of new ventures in the technology industry is to determine whether they are truly making progress in the direction that Ted outlined thirty years ago—a direction that has proved itself to be even more viable today than it was then, in its infancy. Both the IBM PC and the Xerox DocuTech (which is discussed in detail in Chapter Three) achieved that end. These products became multi-billion dollar successes.

The IBM PC was launched to the market on August 12, 1981, one short year from the time the project was approved by the Corporate Management Committee, but it was many years in the making before that. Bringing the IBM PC to market was an amazing feat in a company that, in the words of then-CEO Frank Carey, took "three years and 400 people to do anything." What's more, as a business, it went from zero to $12 billion in five short years.

Chapter Three takes us to Xerox Corporation, where as Executive Vice President of Worldwide Development and Manufacturing, I was responsible for about 26,000 of the company's 100,000+ employees, with about a billion dollars in discretionary development budget. I had 13 direct reports. I was also responsible for coordinating with the Xerox/Fuji joint venture in Japan, known as Fuji Xerox. It was a great experience, and I still have a number of close friends from those Xerox days.

The lessons learned at Xerox were tremendously different from those at IBM, but just as insightful in relation to the development of the principles of Pragmatic Innovation. It has long been a puzzle how Xerox could squander the tremendous inventions that were under its roof at the famed Palo Alto Research Center (Xerox PARC). Few companies in history have invested as much in development of technology and given birth to so many innovative products. The list is long. It includes the personal computer, object-oriented computer languages, print technologies, the facsimile, computer networks, and more. The answer to this question is complex, and yet simple: Xerox was clearly in need of an injection of the principles of Pragmatic Innovation.

My first introduction to Xerox Corporation was through David Kearns, the Chairman and CEO at the time. He came from a sales and marketing background, and he had been with the company from its early founding days. Kearns was energetic, enthusiastic, and passionate. He exerted tremendous leadership with a strong belief in innovation. He had brought Xerox Corporation back from the brink of disaster in the face of the challenge presented by Japanese competitors in the copier world during the late 1970s and into the 1980s. He was a true visionary. During personal conversations with me, he expressed the belief that Xerox was poised to take advantage of the newly evolving digital technology revolution. He knew he needed systems and management help from the outside to break the pattern of failure and to reinvent the copier culture that remained entrenched in old practices that had delivered success in the past but were ill-suited for the new digital age.

Much has been written about how the company failed to capitalize on its amazing inventions, in books such as *Fumbling the Future*[5], and more recently, *In Search of Stupidity*[6]. In 1988, Xerox was embarking on a major journey, a bet-the-company venture, really, transitioning itself from the copier company to The Document Company. You will see in this second example of Pragmatic Innovation in action how we successfully launched an entirely new industry—on-demand printing—and converted a closed company with a closed systems architecture to an open systems company. The Xerox of today does an exceptional job of partnering with third parties to extend the value of its offerings. This transition can be traced back to the deployment of the principles of Pragmatic Innovation in the DocuTech program. Within this success, we will also acknowledge what other elements of Pragmatic Innovation were not embraced as successfully. Just as Carey's

---

5   Fumbling the Future, by Douglas K. Smith and Robert C. Alexander, William Morrow & Company, September 1988.

6   In Search of Stupidity, by Merrill R. (Rick) Chapman, APress, July 2003

departure from IBM impacted the organizational willingness to embrace innovation, the departure of David Kearns impacted the ability of Xerox to fully take advantage of its technology investments. His successor, Paul Allaire, was neither as visionary nor energetic as Kearns, and the company suffered from that. In addition, many in the management team did not necessarily have the drive or desire to support the full potential of Xerox's heritage of innovation.

The Xerox DocuTech Production Publisher was launched in October of 1990 at the Jacob Javits Center in New York, with simultaneous broadcast of the event to sites all over the world. It quickly grew into a multi-billion dollar business that laid the foundation for Xerox's current blockbuster products, such as the Xerox iGen3 color digital press. Amazingly, the Xerox DocuTech—which printed at a startling 135 pages per minute at 600 dots per inch, the fastest black & white laser printer in the world at the time—was in the market a full ten years before a viable competitor emerged.

Another aspect of Xerox Corporation was its willingness to embrace a very diverse workplace. As luck would have it, this dynamic would also forever change my life.

As part of this focus on diversity, several very talented women, including Anne Mulcahy, Diane McGarry, Ursula Burns, and Cristina Salvatierra, were brought into the Corporate mainstream to nurture their eventual success and development. Another key Xerox objective was to ensure diversity in the executive suite. Anne, of course, is the current CEO of Xerox Corporation. Her positive influence and direction following the retirement of Paul Allaire and the departure of his successor as CEO, Rick Thoman, has been outstanding. In many ways, Anne has taken Xerox back to the culture of enthusiasm and innovation fostered by David Kearns. However, the person who influenced me the most during my tenure there was Cristina. She had a successful background in systems sales and management in Los Angeles. She had been named Hispanic Business Woman of the Year in 1987, and she was well on her way to joining Anne and Ursula in leadership positions. Instead, she chose to be my wife and to begin her new career as the mother of our two children. Together, we left Xerox to join a very different industry with a very different approach to our joint lifestyle.

Cristina and Bill at the World Economic Forum in Davos, Switzerland
shortly after leaving Xerox

In Chapter Four, we fly off to Gulfstream Aerospace Corporation, where I was brought in as President & CEO by a leveraged buyout specialist, Teddy Forstmann. Gulfstream was the company that literally created the Jet Set. During that time, we counted most of the world's rich and famous among our clients. But its management structure at the time was not conducive to continued innovation. Forstmann was a forceful entrepreneur who was quite concerned about the reaction of his Limited Partners should refinancing be required. We had a very senior Board who looked like the Who's Who of the Republican Party—George Schultz, Donald Rumsfeld, Drew Lewis, and others. Neither the company nor the industry was known for innovation.

Ted had been impressed with my accomplishments at IBM and Xerox Corporation. He wanted to bring that energy into the company.

At the time, the company's flagship product, the Gulfstream IV, was facing serious competition from its competitor, Canadair, who was talking about introducing a new aircraft that stood to totally eclipse Gulfstream's offerings. Gulfstream, which had never done much competitive benchmarking or industry analysis, was essentially unaware of this competitive threat and in complete denial. We used our no-nonsense approach to Pragmatic Innovation to blend the best of our inside people with information and people from the outside. The result was the hugely successful Gulfstream GV. This was another multi-billion dollar winner that positioned Gulfstream to go public. We also helped establish a new market segment—shared ownership of jets for executive travel. This completely turned Gulfstream's position around, allowed it to proceed with a successful IPO, and met the investors' expectations. Despite the glamour and the rarified air of travel on a Gulfstream jet, this experience introduced me to a management process driven by greed, discrimination, and avarice—a far cry from the level of integrity that I had experience at IBM or Xerox. However, Pragmatic Innovation, as will be shown, ultimately carried the day. This story demonstrates that Pragmatic Innovation can make a difference in both large publicly owned organizations and in the entrepreneurial environment—as well as across industries.

By its very nature, the Gulfstream chapter is chock-full of stories about the rich and famous we met along the way. But more importantly, by now I knew I had landed on a process that worked. It as clear that I could apply this process anywhere to stimulate innovation and to generate business success.

In Chapters Five and Six, we will see how this same process was applied in several other companies, some of which are clearly smaller and represent different and less innovative industries. One of the most exciting of these was NEBS[7], which readers might remember as the dominant mail order forms company of the last century serving very small businesses. By applying the principals of Pragmatic Innovation at NEBS, we were able to discover that most new very small businesses (VSBs)—a key target market for this company—were woman-owned. We also found that those entrepreneurial businesswomen had a very different set of requirements as compared to traditional buyers of forms. This new market segment wanted color and customization, a new concept for an old-style company with little innovation in its history. By meeting this need, NEBS was able to introduce an innovative spirit and to set new directions for successful growth based on our collection and analysis of data. This demonstrates a key element of the Pragmatic Innovation process.

One of the other companies highlighted, Moore Corporation, has since been absorbed into the world's largest printer, RR Donnelley. At the time I was engaged, we were facing a crossroads, needing to make a decision about whether to embrace Pragmatic Innovation or drive for a consolidation strategy to boost the stock price without having to invest in any new innovation. As it turned out, the CEO preferred the consolidation strategy. That is where it became crystal clear to me that innovation cannot proceed without top level support and vision. This was a classic case of lost opportunity when innovation is not embraced.

Our experience with Proamics provides an opportunity to highlight some of my work with startup organizations. The full innovation process was applied to a ten million dollar break-even software company that was able to double its size, raise money, be acquired, and go public in a brief two-year period. This proved that Pragmatic Innovation can work for entry level companies as well as large organizations.

---

7   New England Business Services

It was in working with these companies that I began to formalize my thinking relative to the types of leaders that are most effective in developing and nurturing business innovation. Also, my experiences there validated my belief that without the appropriate leadership, innovation often stops. This is especially true when key innovators move on to other assignments. This often results in the culture of Pragmatic Innovation failing to prevail in favor of sliding back to "business as usual." It is my hope and belief that by sharing these personal experiences, I will be able to help others avoid some of the challenges that are inevitably faced on the road to innovative success.

Chapter Seven documents progress to date at NEPS[8]—not to be confused with NEBS. NEPS is an interesting technology and services company. For a period of time, I served as CEO of NEPS, a company that was at one time the Emerging Technologies division of Moore Corporation. With Moore's acquisition by RR Donnelley—or some would say RR Donnelley's acquisition by Moore, since the Moore management team ended up running the company!—NEPS founder Denise Miano was able to spin the company back out, including the retention of ownership of all IP. The spin-out came with its challenges, however, most of which were financial. I worked with NEPS using the principles of Pragmatic Innovation for nearly two years, and the company is now beginning to see exciting results.

Chapter Eight summarizes the insight and tools presented in the book. It lays out an easy-to-follow, step-by-step approach that any business in any industry can use to deploy Pragmatic Innovation. We include a range of tools and suggestions that can be easily modified to meet organization-specific needs. I also include examples from several innovative consulting arrangements where I have applied Pragmatic Innovation. Through the deployment of its principles,

---

8   The company was originally known as New England Programming Services; thus the acronym.

I have been able to assist many companies in their journey to a long-term culture of innovation.

Our final chapter documents the beginning stages of our latest Pragmatic Innovation deployment, QWK2LRN, a revolutionary approach to a one-to-one computing initiative primarily designed for primary and secondary schools. It is our first public sector deployment of Pragmatic Innovation. This initiative is benefiting significantly from the experience we have had over the last 20 years with this process. It is an ideal closing chapter, because it closes the loop on so many things.

Our key partner in this project is IBM. So while I started my career 20 years ago at Big Blue, I am now working with the company again in this exciting joint venture. It also brings to fruition the vision of Ted Nelson from all those years ago, bringing the story full circle.

It is our hope that this book will change the way you think about your business. Our aim is to help you bring a new spirit of innovation—and a new burst of growth—to your company. I also hope you will enjoy the stories I share from my journey in business, with its many twists and turns, that has helped me to develop a process that truly works.

Keep in mind that the innovation environment is a moving target. There are always new developments on the horizon, requiring innovators to keep their eyes open for changes that can impact their innovation efforts.

One example of this is documented in the book *Wikinomics: How Mass Collaboration Changes Everything*[9]. The authors explain how massive online communities are revolutionizing business today in the development of everything from encyclopedias to jetliners. As an innovator, I will be keeping a close personal eye on this trend—and others—as we continue to work with companies to invent the future.

---

9   Wikinomics: The Expanded Edition, by Don Tapscott and Anthony D. Williams, Portfolio Hardcover, April 2008

CHAPTER 2

The IBM PC Story:
Teaching the Elephant to Dance

*"Leaders are visionaries with a poorly developed sense of fear
and no concept of the odds against them. They make the impossible happen."*

DR. ROBERT JARVIK

I t is completely natural for humans to resist change and to fight to stay in their comfort zone. It is in this regard, perhaps, that large companies—and many medium to small companies—are most human. IBM, during my days there, was certainly no exception. . Much has been written about how the IBM PC was brought to market, but the story

29

has never before been told from the inside perspective. What are the dynamics inside a large company such as IBM in the late 1970's that typically prevent innovations like the PC from ever seeing the light of day? How close did that come to actually happening and why? Who did what to whom from the time the idea was first floated until the product got out the door, and beyond? As I look back over my IBM years, I am still amazed at some of the things that happened. I am sure you will be, as well. It is those inside details that really demonstrate why Pragmatic Innovation works in some circumstances and why it can fail in others.

In addition to the interesting, and often never-before-told, autobiographical and historical details addressed in this chapter, the IBM story is a great example of how Pragmatic Innovation can allow you to do things differently in your own business—often extremely exciting new things. What has really come home to me as I have been working on this book is that IBM eventually made all the classic mistakes that companies make, and those mistakes ultimately constrained the business and its ability to innovate going forward. This took place after the company's initial success with the PC program due to the influence of the philosophy of Pragmatic Innovation and the leadership of then-CEO Frank Carey. During these early days of the IBM PC, IBM "taught the elephant to dance," but like many big companies, they then took away its dancing lessons and constrained it to simply dancing the waltz, over and over again.

From Zero to $12 Billion in Five Years

I started my career right out of school with IBM, and I am extremely grateful for the experiences that were afforded me there. I learned a great deal while at IBM. I was able to spread my wings and accomplish much more than I ever dreamed I could. It was there that the philosophy of Pragmatic Innovation began to evolve for me. By applying that philosophy to my work at IBM, I like to think that I made some interesting and significant contributions to the company, and to the industry, not the least of which was bringing the IBM PC to market.

It is not often that one gets the opportunity to take a business from zero to $12 billion dollars in five short years—and get recognition for it from your industry. In 1990, Bill Gates and I were honored by *PC Magazine* as being responsible for delivering the best hardware and software of the previous decade, and that was saying plenty.

Gates and Lowe

Much has been written over the last quarter century about the IBM PC story. I especially watched with interest all of the press coverage in 2006 as the 25th anniversary of the IBM PC was observed. The story has been told and retold. As often happens, much of what you hear is legend—not necessarily fact. I was there for all of it—the hallowed halls of the IBM Corporate Management Committee; the skunk works of the famous "Dirty Dozen" in Boca Raton, Florida; the coast-to-coast flights for meetings with Gates and his team; the wild ride up, and ultimately, the slippery slope down which IBM slid as it began to revert to form.

So let me take you on a trip down memory lane, sharing my perspective on the IBM PC story. Along the way, we will see what worked—and what didn't. We will explore how the philosophy of Pragmatic Innovation played a huge role in bringing to market one of the most revolutionary products of all time. We will also see how IBM fell into all of the classic innovation traps that Harvard Professor and author Rosabeth Moss Kantor outlined in her November 2006 Harvard Business Review article.[1]

- They moved the innovator (me) out of the innovating group to another position.

- They began to do things for the base business which really hurt the ability for the new business to do what it needed to do to succeed.

- They eventually constrained the new business by favoring the internal sales and marketing channel, disenfranchising the new sales channel we had built.

- They took money away from the program to support the struggling base business.

- They required the PC business to use internal technology at a cost that was too high to produce a competitive product.

- They corrupted the software that was being developed for the second generation, and then made decisions regarding

---

1 *Innovation: The Classic Traps,* by Rosabeth Moss Kantor, Harvard Business Review, November 2006

the UNIX operating system that ultimately destroyed the relationship with Microsoft.

Despite its initial successes, the IBM PC story is a classic example of Pragmatic Innovation gone wrong. It is a powerful story of how this kind of innovation can make extremely good things happen, but it is also a powerful story about how a large company tends to make critical decisions while looking in the rearview mirror based on the business metrics that delivered its early success. The real lesson the IBM experience teaches is that you not only have to leverage Pragmatic Innovation to bring innovative products and services to market, but you have to foster a culture that allows it to continue beyond the initial success.

In his book *Teaching the Elephant to Dance*[2], change guru Dr. James Belasco says, "Shackled, like powerful elephants, to the past, organizations rob themselves of the ingenuity required to meet new competitive challenges." In the case of the IBM PC, we definitely taught the elephant to dance, but ultimately, IBM took away the elephant's dancing lessons, thereby constraining the organization's ability to innovate. Here is the story.

How It All Began

I joined IBM in 1962 as a product test engineer in Endicott, New York, after graduating with a Bachelor of Science degree in Physics from Lafayette College in Easton, Pennsylvania. During my tenure with IBM, I proved out the other often-used tongue-in-cheek meaning of the acronym—"**I**'ve **B**een **M**oved"—by moving 17 times for the company.

---

2   *Teaching the Elephant to Dance: The Manager's Guide to Empowering Change*, by James A. Belasco, Crown, May 12, 1990

Lowe in front of The Lafayette Leopard on campus in Easton PA

I was fascinated with the opportunities IBM presented. I had done my undergraduate research on the somewhat esoteric subject of electron-spin resonance (ESR), a spectroscopic technique which detects unpaired electrons in organic or inorganic compounds. I was not sure where it was going to take me, but I thought perhaps I could make a difference in the field of computing. I remember growing up, when my father worked as an accountant for Dixie Cup, that it used to take the entire month to manually process the company's payroll. By the early 1960's when I joined IBM, its computers could do the same work in a week—although the computer was operating 24/7 and often broke down. In fact, the abysmal reliability record of these early computers prompted a letter from the Boeing CEO to then IBM leader Thomas J. Watson, stating, "If our planes were as reliable as your computers, would you be willing to fly on them?" That led to a significant change in IBM reliability, and I was ready to see if I could help take it even further. In the context of the larger world, it was about this time that President Kennedy challenged the American people to send a man to the moon by the end of the decade. For me, both of these events provided object lessons about what could be achieved if the blinders are removed and a challenge is given to deliver innovation in a big way.

The PC story really began for me, though, in 1974 when I was Director of Technology for the General Systems Division. The company was investing heavily in what it dubbed "Future Systems Technology," an attempt to migrate its semiconductor technology from what consisted of somewhere between three and ten circuits per semiconductor to a more densely populated, liquid-cooled package to be used in high end systems. At the same time, the company was beginning to realize it needed to move down-market, adding lower end systems to its portfolio. I was tasked with identifying how this technology could be used for these lower end systems. When we spoke about low-end systems, we were considering products like the System/34, a lower-cost approach to distributive data processing that later would be called a mini-computer. It was ultimately brought to market in 1977 for a price tag of about $50,000—equivalent to nearly $200,000, inflation-adjusted to today's dollars. Pricey, but much less pricey than its mainframe brothers and sisters.

The objective of Future Systems Technology was to build a set of replacement systems for the future that were as highly integrated as possible. IBM undertook a major effort in East Fishkill, New York, to develop technology that packaged multiple chips in complex modules. We are talking about a very complex system with dense packages that generated a tremendous amount of heat. As a result, Future Systems Technology would require liquid cooling to dissipate that heat. This was a huge investment for IBM, and its proponents asserted that the future of the company hinged on its success. IBM committed billions of dollars to this effort.

But not everyone supported the concept. I remember speaking with a number of division presidents, who at least privately questioned the strategy. One in particular was Ted Papes, who ultimately went on to become president and chief executive officer of early online services provider Prodigy. When I asked him why he didn't make his voice heard, he said, "You don't understand, Bill. I am in a position where I cannot afford to take on certain issues."

Ted was extremely politically astute. I remember being with him in England some years later when the press wanted to take our photos. We were both division presidents at the time. As I sat down to have my photo taken, Ted stood up. He said, "Never have your picture taken sitting down. You have to look like you are a man of action." Yet in the earlier case of Future Systems Technology, the man of action was certainly not Ted.

At the time Future Systems Technology was being discussed, IBM, like many companies, mandated that all of its products must use IBM technology. It was anathema that anyone would even consider using third party solutions, as strange as that sounds today. As Harvard Professor Henry Chesbrough so eloquently explained in his 2003 defining work on the concept of Open Innovation,[3] "internal R&D was viewed as a strategic asset and even a barrier to competitive entry … Only large companies with significant resources and long-term research programs could compete." IBM certainly followed that model, along with many of its peers of the day, jealously guarding its technology and operating in a very internally-focused manner. While the company was certainly aware of competing technologies in the marketplace, it was imperious about believing that what it had to offer was the best.

Changing Market Dynamics

But market forces were beginning to move faster than IBM. I could see things happening outside the company that were destined to have a huge impact on both the price of technology and our ability to compete long term. Key among these was Hewlett-Packard's introduction in 1972 of the HP-35,

3   *Open Innovation*, by Henry Chesbrough, Harvard Business School Press, 2003

the world's first electronic slide rule. It was very futuristic at the time. In fact, the 1972 user manual stated: "Our objective in developing the HP-35 was to give you a high precision portable electronic slide rule. We thought you'd like to have something only fictional heroes like James Bond, Walter Mitty or Dick Tracy are supposed to own."

The HP-35 was a calculator brought to market at a time when most calculators, even expensive desktop versions, only had four functions—add, subtract, multiply, and divide. It was HP's first pocket calculator, according to the Museum of HP Calculators[4]. The HP-35 was the first pocket calculator with transcendental functions, the first with Reverse Polish Notation (RPN); it was priced at just over $1,000. As a comparison, IBM's lowest priced product at the time weighed in at some $25,000.

HP had previously introduced a larger scientific calculator, the HP-9100, and the Museum reports:

> Based on marketing studies done at the time, the HP-9100 was the "right" size and price for a scientific calculator. The studies showed little or no interest in a pocket device. However [HP founder] Bill Hewlett thought differently. He began the development of a "shirt pocket-sized HP-9100" on an accelerated schedule. It was a risky project involving several immature technologies. ... Based on [another] marketing study, it was believed that they might sell 50,000 units. It turned out that the marketing study was wrong by an order of magnitude. Within the first few months they received orders exceeding their guess as to the total market size. General Electric alone placed an order for 20,000 units.

In view of this and other market developments, I concluded that Future Systems Technology was too expensive for use in low-end systems. But I

---

4   On the Web at http://www.hpmuseum.org/hp35.htm

was certainly the Lone Ranger in vocalizing that position. There were some powerful people who believed that Future Systems Technology was the answer—not only for our next generation of mainframes, but for low-end systems such as the System/34 as well. Perhaps the most powerful of the Future Systems proponents was John Opel, who had just been appointed to the role of President of IBM, under then-Chairman Frank Carey. I later learned that he was chosen over another executive, George B. "Spike" Beitzel, based on his role in Future Systems Technology and the progress this particular project had made under his leadership.

My position was that using Future Systems Technology in low end products such as the System/34 would increase their cost by a factor of two or three. I had no beef with the use of Future Systems Technology at the high end—that wasn't my concern at the time. You can imagine what a risky position that was in those days, as evidenced by the reluctance of Ted Papes to speak out against Future Systems Technology. But I was a young renegade and didn't know any better. I was very lucky to be working for and mentored by C. B. "Jack" Rogers, who was the General Manager of GSD in Atlanta at the time and one of the more open-minded and supportive managers I have had during my long career.

With Jack's encouragement, I put together a presentation outlining my position. When Opel visited Atlanta just two weeks into his tenure as President, I was given the opportunity to deliver that presentation. As I went through the discussion, I could see Opel becoming increasingly angry—even red in the face. I was just 33 years old and had three little kids to support. I thought to myself, "This is looking like a great career starter." I figured that my days were numbered, but I felt strongly enough about my position that I had no regrets about presenting it, regardless of the outcome.

About three days after that presentation, I got a call from Jack's executive assistant, who said, "Bill, you have to go to Armonk to make your presentation to Allen Krowe, CFO of the company."

To say I was surprised was an understatement. I had never been to Armonk, and I had never met anyone like Krowe. But I did have the presence of mind to ask if I could look at Jack's files on the subject. To my shock, the top letter in the file was from John Opel, recommending that Rogers "tie a can to that kid Lowe for giving bad staff advice."

In the meeting, Krowe said, "We just had a meeting about a month ago with the Chairman, and we have decided to put another $3 billion into Future Systems Technology. Would you like to tell Mr. Carey your story?"

"No sir," I said. "Nonetheless, my position is still that Future Systems Technology may work for the high end, but it will not work for the low end."

He said, "So you are telling me that you think IBM has lost sight of affordability in terms of our fixed costs?"

"Yes, sir, that is exactly what I am saying, from a low-end perspective."

A week or so later, much to my relief, Rogers informed me that it had been decided that I was providing good staff advice after all and was working in the best interests of the company. I then believed I would live to make a few more moves with IBM. As further validation of my position, shortly after that I was invited by Allen Krowe to a meeting with about 50 other people where it was decided to scrap Future Systems Technology because IBM had lost sight of fixed cost affordability. This was just a few brief weeks after it had been decided to invest an additional $3 billion in the project!

This was the first time in my career that I had gone against the grain of "business as usual" based on the philosophy of Pragmatic Innovation—although I didn't have a name for it at the time. It certainly was not the last, as we shall see. It was also my entree into the senior executive suite and the launching pad for my career at IBM. Spike Bietzel asked me to become his new executive assistant, and he also asked me to join a task force that was being established to set a new direction for the company. I would be representing the low end of the product range in this work.

Dogged by the DOJ

The other dynamic that was at work here was the 1956 U.S. Department of Justice (DOJ) Consent Decree under which IBM was operating. The Decree settled an antitrust suit brought by the U.S. government in 1952. In signing the Decree, IBM agreed, among other things, to end its rental-only policy and sell machines at prices that were reasonable in comparison to rental rates; to allow others to buy parts to repair or upgrade its machines; and to maintain machines reconfigured by customers or third parties. IBM also promised to operate any services business it owned as arm's length subsidiaries. As a result, IBM ultimately established an independent equipment leasing business and allowed third parties to maintain IBM equipment. This also led to other spin-off businesses, including plug-compatible processors and peripherals. It was in this environment that IBM was forced to pay more attention to the outside world, and the Decree created an environment more conducive to the internal initiatives that would ultimately lead to the birth of the IBM PC.

As with many things government, though, the consent decree process dragged out for years, with the Department of Justice seemingly finding an endless array of applications of the Decree to keep IBM under its thumb. These battles were still going on in the mid-1970s during the period that I was weighing in on the Future Systems Technology battle. IBM continued to argue to the DOJ that it was serving its customers better by using only its own hardware technology, internally developed software, and IBM sales and service as an integrated product offering. The company did not believe that the best interests of its customers could be served by publishing its hardware and software interfaces, thereby opening them up to third parties.

Still fresh from my apparent success on the Future Systems Technology battlefield and with a new-born confidence engendered by my role on the task force, I was prompted to present yet another controversial proposition—that IBM split the company in two in order to attempt a settlement before the latest anti-trust trial started. I was the youngest person on the task force, by far, but when Spike Beitzel asked the group the "what if" question, I was the only one that raised my hand, suggesting that we split the company based on software lines—with the System 370 in one company and everything else in the other.

This proposal was approved by the IBM Corporate Management Committee and actually presented to the government by Bietzel and former U.S. Attorney Nicholas Katzenbach, who had joined IBM to lead the DOJ fight. The government countered, saying we needed to split the company into three. Again, I was the only one to raise my hand, suggesting that we break out the OS/DOS operating system. That proposal was rejected by IBM, and ultimately the company told the DOJ that it could not support a three-way split as being in the interest of our shareholders.

Although these proposals didn't go anywhere with the government, my participation and the courage of my convictions further increased my political capital within the inner sanctum of the IBM Corporate Management Committee.

Through all of this, although we didn't realize it at the time, the groundwork had been laid for a dramatic change in the world of computing.

Taking a Big Company Small

My next move, in 1976, was back to Atlanta as Director of Software and Architecture for General Systems Division (GSD). I still felt we needed to look at product development differently, and I believed that there was an opportunity to compete with HP in an area that IBM considered almost beneath it—the HP-35 electronic slide rule was slick, and selling like hotcakes. Surely if we did this right, we could enter the low end and win big, though maybe not as low as the HP-35. As I said earlier, our entry level product, the System/25, was priced at $25,000—which certainly limited us in terms of the range of companies we could influence. Even so, we lost money on every one we sold because our overhead was so high, mostly because of our direct sales costs.

My team began modeling all new low-end products with vendor technology purchased from outside of IBM. For each low-end product, we scoured Radio Shack and other sources for components. We demonstrated that we could build these products for about one-third the price and in 40 percent of the time that our traditional product development processes required. We did this by simply sourcing components and technology from outside the company. In 1978, this led to my being reassigned to Boca Raton as Lab Director. In that role, it would be my job, among other things, to assemble a small team to track the emerging micro business and to determine when we should be producing micro-based products using external technology. Based on my experiences thus far with the Corporate Management Committee, one thing was clear. I would need to have my ducks in a row. I needed facts, and I needed them fast. My team was looking outside IBM to develop a new perspective.

Thus, we pored over the emerging computing hobbyist magazines. We visited Radio Shack and the executive management of ComputerLand, Sears Business Centers. and other outlets. We kept our finger on the pulse of what was happening in this newly developing "micro" market, keeping a special eye on what Apple was doing. It was exhilarating, actually, after wandering the hallowed halls of IBM for so long, and the activity breathed new life into the team, a skunk works operation, really, ultimately dubbed "The Dirty Dozen."

Members of the Dirty Dozen, in addition to me, included Dennis Gibbs, Joe Bauman, Burke Veeley, Lew Eggebrecht, Jack Sams, Noel Fallwell, Patty McHugh, Jan Winston, David Bradley, Bob Wolfson, and Dan Wilkie.

So as 1980 rang in, the bell tolled for me as well—we had the opportunity to present some of our work to various IBM executives. Ultimately, the project was drawn to Frank Carey's attention. Around the same time, Atari approached IBM with a proposal that IBM develop the operating system for Atari's computers. I was asked to attend a meeting of the Corporate Management Committee to give my opinion. I told them I did not think it was appropriate.

I said, "We know how to build a micro-based product in Boca, and we could do it in a year."

Carey said, "You're on. Come back in two weeks and tell me how you are going to do it." This was late July of 1980.

I remember Carey saying, after learning that many of our software developers were moonlighting by creating software for Apple for publication in its "Apple Orchard Magazine," "Bill, we need to recapture the hearts and minds of our developers." At the time, you could submit software to the magazine, and if it was published, you received some level of remuneration. I think even he was becoming a little frustrated with the IBM process, because I recall him saying, "It takes three years and 400 people to do anything at

IBM." Perhaps he saw this project as a way to address both concerns.

Based on other successes with my team in Boca Raton, I was sure The Dirty Dozen was ready to proceed. I believed we could get it done, and the team and I got to work.

The PC That Almost Didn't Happen

So we were back in two weeks for the historic CMC meeting of August 8, 1980, with a very thorough presentation and a system prototype. Our sponsor at the meeting was Jack Rogers, who was my boss at the time and the General Manager of IBM's General Systems Division in Atlanta. We were prepared and ready to go, but the GSD staff began talking about the IBM store concept, which ate up a lot of time. Rogers was still unsure whether he even wanted the PC subject on the table. At the end of the meeting, I truly thought we were not going to be able to present. But Carey said, "I thought you were coming back with a micro proposal."

I said, "Yes, sir, we are ready. We can even give you a demonstration."

So we were on, and our presentation went two hours beyond the scheduled meeting end time. This was very unusual at IBM in those days, especially for the Corporate Management Committee. As a rule, they stuck religiously to scheduled meeting times.

During our presentation, we outlined for the Corporate Management Committee exactly what we proposed to do. In those days, our presentations were all handwritten. They were written on full-sized easel charts, and we sent them to a blueprint house to make small copies for handouts. I have donated what I believe is the only remaining copy of this presentation in existence to the library of my alma mater, Lafayette College. Several pages will be used with this text,

As you can see, we believed we had a significant opportunity, much in the way Bill Hewlett had believed HP had an opportunity with the HP-35—and as you will see, we underestimated just as badly! But the challenges were many, crossing the product development and delivery spectrum, including the fact that we could not undertake this important project with the existing workload and allocated resources at the lab in Boca Raton. I was asked by Howie Davidson, GM of Boca, to put this latter item on the chart. I included it, although I felt this was just another indication of how wary people were about taking on a "maverick" program.

At the time, we were not calling this a personal computer. It was simply a micro-based product.

In the two weeks Carey gave us, we put together a proposed system architecture.

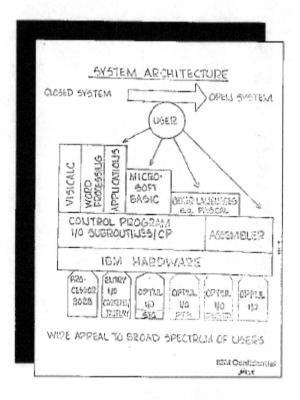

We were looking for a product that would have wide appeal to a broad spectrum of users. We were not just targeting engineers or information technology professionals. We could see from our external market research that there was a growing need for a micro-based product that was perhaps a little more robust than the Apple II and could be used in both business and technical applications. We also thought there would be hobbyists and what you might define today as "geeks" who would buy these systems.

I have subsequently discussed this with Apple's Steve Jobs. He told me that when he started Apple Computer, his passion was to build a computer for the educational environment. This highlighted a significant difference between the IBM PC and the Apple II and early Macintosh. We were building a product we thought would be helpful for business people, despite the fact that it would be called a personal computer. The applications we chose, the way we choose to lay out the architecture, and the way we presented information on the screen reflected that choice; it was more characteristic of what you would find in business. Apple, on the other hand, was more geared to kids and schools; thus you saw a high volume of gaming and educational software. We focused on applications like spreadsheets and word processing. Jobs believed that his products would ultimately evolve into a better business machine because of their educational roots. We started out with a design intent that reflected business needs.

When you look at the architecture diagram above, *it had virtually no IBM content!* We had used the model that the Boca Raton technical team and I had been using for the previous three years—use third-party technology in low-end products to produce them better, faster, and more cost-effectively than the competition—and certainly, more cost effectively than IBM could ever do. To date, our systems had always been closed systems. But we knew that for this product to be successful, it had to be an open system. This was the first formal proposal I made in my career that embodied the no-nonsense principles of Pragmatic Innovation. When you think about it, the proposed architecture was pretty close to the product that was actually launched. But as you can imagine, there was a bit of a battle getting over that Open Systems hurdle. You will also note that the architecture allowed for a number of different peripherals (noted as Optional I/O[5] on the diagram), making the proposed product configurable by the users. This next chart shows how we thought that would work.

5 I/O—Input/Output

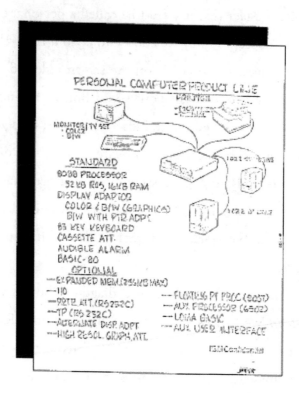

We were planning to use a whole 16 kilobytes of memory! That was a concession to the high cost of random access memory (RAM) at the time. IBM was charging $1 million per megabyte, and we were able to negotiate the cost down to $32,000 per megabyte for this program with Frank Carey's support. Nonetheless, 16 kilobytes wasn't much memory. While people could upgrade, we felt we needed to keep the entry price low on the base model.

Our market research indicated that Apple's cost to manufacture the Apple II was about $1,200 to sell the unit at $1,595. We then worked with an outside consultant[6] who informed us that the manufacturing cost for the

---

6   This consultant, whose name is lost in the annals of history somewhere, was chosen after I interviewed a number of candidates. He was extremely credible and delivered facts, not opinions. When we stated we believed memory would cost X on the open market, he was quick to reply that no, it would cost Y—that is what Apple is paying—and here is where you buy it. He was an internal resource for Boca, never presented to the CMC, and they were no doubt unaware of his existence. He did, however, provide us with the

Apple II was actually $230. That demonstrated how far off the mark we were in terms of our perspective on what could be done. Using our Pragmatic Innovation principles and the outside advisor to help us understand and communicate Apple's cost structure, we were able to reduce our internal cost estimate from $1,300 to $325.

Finally, and probably most interesting of all, were our projections about how many units could be sold. This is where we had a great deal in common with Bill Hewlett. We thought we could sell 221,600 units worldwide, through all channels, in the first four years of the program. We thought we were being aggressive—keep in mind that with that forecast, we were forecasting more installed PCs than IBM's total installed system inventory at that time. Doubling the population of IBM computers, I thought, was big enough.

indisputable facts that were required to argue our case to the CMC.

This is also where the DOJ antitrust suits loop back into the picture. Remember that the DOJ was unhappy with the closed nature of IBM's systems and wanted us to publish interfaces so that others could participate in IBM's success. This entire micro program, which was code-named Manhattan, was designed around an open architecture that would encourage hardware providers and software developers to design for the system and to participate in our success. This was even more open than the Apple II. We did recommend committing to publishing and maintaining our hardware and software interfaces.

I personally met with a number of potential channel partners, including ComputerLand and Sears Business Centers, during this period to explore their willingness to participate. The truth was, they were not excited. They did not trust that IBM would be a good long-term partner, and they were concerned that they would invest heavily, as would other developers, and then IBM would pull the plug. Their position was, unequivocally, "You must commit to the industry that you will publish and maintain the interfaces, and that you will support them on an ongoing basis so we can feel safe making an investment."

The computer stores also wanted the right to service the computers—that is where they made a significant chunk of their money. Historically, IBM had been a closed environment, not only from an R&D and manufacturing perspective, but also from a sales and service perspective. So the third-party sales and service aspect was another huge divergence from tradition for this program. Of course, one proposed channel was the IBM Stores the company proposed to open, and product sold through that channel could utilize IBM sales and service.

Where the Rubber Meets the Road

You can just imagine the reaction of the Corporate Management Committee to this proposal, especially the guarantee to deliver software and hardware interfaces to facilitate development by third-party developers. There was significant discussion centered around the three key questions that the Corporate Management Committee always asked about new programs:

- Will we be competitive?

- Will we make money?

- Will we be proud of this product?

In the end, Frank Carey was willing to make the investment, and his vote carried the day. It was clear that he wanted to move forward with our project, and in particular, he was supportive of our desire to move to open systems and to share our interfaces with the industry. Without that support at the highest level, the program never would have happened.

When you talk about teaching the elephant to dance, it was the most amazing thing that IBM would move forward with a project of this nature. Here we were in front of the Corporate Management Committee showing them numbers the likes of which they had never seen before: low costs, fewer people, a very tight project schedule, and doubling IBM's computer installed base in four short years!

Carey threw his considerable weight behind making sure that we faced as few internal obstacles as possible as we worked through the inevitable IBM bureaucracy. In those days, you had to obtain concurrence from a wide variety of people throughout the organization to get things done. If someone gave you a "non-concurrence," it was your responsibility to get that removed or resolved in order to move forward. Many good programs died ignominious deaths as a result of that policy. Carey said, "Bill, not everyone is going to concur with you. If you get a non-concurrence and you think it is wrong, I will give you access to the Corporate Management Committee within 24 hours to get a resolution." The word must have gotten out, because we went for the entire year of the development of the PC with no non-concurrences—which was almost unheard of, especially for a project this controversial. Because of Frank Carey's support, we achieved the program goals.

Then President John Opel, on the other hand, did not attend the August 8, 1980, Corporate Management Committee meeting, so I went to see him personally, offering to give him a personal review of the project in his office. As I stated earlier, we had some history over our differing positions on Future Systems Technology; I was a bit of a burr under his saddle. He would have preferred that I go to some lab somewhere to build something and stop "fooling around with the Corporate Management Committee."

During that private review session, I told him that we had chosen Microsoft and Bill Gates as our primary software partner. He had heard how young Gates was and that he had dropped out of Harvard. His first thought was that I had lost my senses partnering with this unknown company, but then he realized that Mary Gates was Bill's mother. He had worked with her on a National United Fund campaign and had even been in touch with her after first hearing about our plan to partner with Microsoft. He agreed that he would support that arrangement, adding, "You are telling me to not rain on your parade."

I responded, "No, sir."

He said, "Don't worry about it, Lowe. Just get it done."

I have spent a lot of time with Bill Gates at different times, and I know that he was in constant contact with his mother. She had a very big influence on him, and he obviously held her in extremely high regard. They were very close, and in this case, she performed a valuable service for both her son and the industry through her relationship with Opel.

Of course, in an organization like IBM, politics always run rampant. At the time, Jack Kuehler, President of the General Technology Division, was making all of the technology decisions. IBM had earlier failed with the System/25, which, as I mentioned before, was a business computer priced at $25,000. Jack thought highly of Motorola's technology. He put together a team in Kingston, New York, to develop a competitive alternative to our PC, taking a traditional, proprietary approach. His team clearly did not have any understanding of what would be required from a channel and service perspective to make this type of initiative successful. I believe he even took his proposal to the Corporate Management Committee, but it was not approved.

For Kuehler, this was another political ploy to regain control. Meanwhile, my team believed that Intel was easier to deal with than Motorola. We also held the position that the real decision was whether to use an 8-bit or 16-bit processor. In order to achieve the aggressive schedule we had set for ourselves, we made decisions quickly, stuck with them, and made them work.

The Corporate Management Committee knew IBM needed to get into the low end market. The failure of the System/25 combined with Kuehler's failed takeover attempt heightened its interest in taking a different approach.

The Life Boat Rule

We also had access to an IBM financial advisor, Burke Veeley. Based on his analysis and mine, we concluded that we could not use the full IBM ratio sheet and deliver a competitive product. When you are building a product in a company, whether it is NEPS today or IBM back then, there are a set of financial realities—fixed costs associated with paying the program's share of administrative costs. In another early example of Pragmatic Innovation, I proposed treating my project like a life boat. That meant only allowing into that life boat resources—and associated costs—that specifically contributed to the end result. That was the only way the financial metrics would work for this new business, and that was how we got to the $325 manufacturing cost. We obtained the support to operate in that manner.

The DOS Dilemma

A critical element of this program was the need to source an operating system. We had already been in touch with a small firm out of Seattle called Microsoft—in fact, I think it was three people at the time, Bill Gates, Steve Ballmer, and Paul Allen. Jack Sams first met with Gates shortly before the August 8th Corporate Management Committee meeting. At that meeting, we showed Gates and his team the prototype of the proposed product that we would demonstrate to the Corporate Management Committee two weeks later. It was not, of course, a fully functioning computer, but we were able to show them images of dancing people on the screen, and in form, it was essentially identical to the first PC. I met with Bill and Steve for the first time about ten days later in White Plains.

During July and August of 1980, Jack Sams, who was leading the Dirty Dozen's software team, had met several times with Gates and Ballmer to talk about software, ultimately discussing the development by Microsoft of programming language interpreters/compilers for the PC. Gates agreed to supply BASIC and other software development tools. We also asked Microsoft to provide CP/M as an operating system. Gates, however, informed us that Digital Research owned that intellectual property.

So Sams' next stop was a meeting with Gary Kildall of Digital Research in Monterey, California, a meeting arranged by Bill Gates. Kildall had a Ph.D. in Computer Science from the University of Washington; interestingly, he and Gates both grew up in Seattle. According to various historical accounts, Gates and Kildall were both fascinated with computers and first crossed paths when they worked on the same DEC PDP-10 computer system. Their mutual interest in computers had caused them to stay in touch.

Kildall, who joined the Navy in 1972 and was assigned to the Naval Postgraduate School in Monterey, California, reportedly purchased an Intel 4004 microprocessor chip set for use in his classroom. The 4004 was Intel's first microprocessor and, in fact, the first microprocessor in the world. It was programmable, handled 4-bit words, and contained 2,250 transistors. As a result of this work, Kildall was the first person to interface a disk system to a microcomputer and to create an operating system for it. This changed what had previously been a circuit designed for process control applications into a fully functional computer. With this development, microcomputers could now perform tasks previously done only on minicomputers and mainframes. The world changed dramatically because of his work.

After his discharge from the Navy in 1976, Kildall remained in the Monterey area and founded the company that would ultimately be known as Digital Research. There he developed the CP/M operating system. When he was approached by IBM in 1980 as a result of the Gates introduction, he flatly refused IBM's offer to license CP/M[7]. So Sams went back to Microsoft to ask them to develop or find an operating system that this project could use. Paul Allen licensed a CP/M clone, QDOS[8] from Seattle Computer Products, reportedly for a sum of $50,000, and PC-DOS was ultimately born.

When Kildall later analyzed PC-DOS, he concluded that there were serious copyright infringements. His attorneys, however, told him that the new field of software copyright infringement was not clear enough to guarantee pursuit

---

7   The story behind the story on this one is that Kildall went flying instead of attending the meeting, leaving his wife, an attorney, to run the meeting. She and IBM could not come to terms on the nondisclosure agreement IBM required, and the discussions never even got underway.

8   QDOS stood for Quick and Dirty Operating System

of a successful legal action. Kildall then approached IBM, threatening legal action, and as a result, IBM agreed to offer CP/M-86 as an option for the PC in return for a release of liability.[9]

The IBM PC Goes to Market

I won't go into detail about the early negotiations with Microsoft in this book because that topic has been covered many times in other writings.

Once we were given the appropriate staffing in the Boca Raton lab to accommodate the project, we began our work in earnest. By January of 1981, we had begun calling the product the IBM Personal Computer. In June of that year, *InfoWorld Magazine* published an article containing details about the product, scheduled for launch in August—within the one year promised to Frank Carey.

One major change in the product from its original architecture, implemented at the insistence of Microsoft, was the upgrade from 16 kilobytes of memory to 64 kilobytes. That made it equivalent to the Apple II, and according to Microsoft, that level of memory was the absolute minimum to ensure adequate functionality.

The first IBM Personal Computers rolled off the assembly line in July of 1981.

On August 12, 1981, the IBM Personal Computer was formally announced at the Waldorf-Astoria Hotel in New York City, and in Boca Raton, Florida. We announced it as the IBM Personal Computer, model 5150; it featured a 4.77 MHz Intel 8088 CPU, 64 kilobytes of RAM (expandable to 256 kilobytes), 40 kilobytes of ROM, one 5.25-inch floppy drive (160 kilobyte capacity), and was priced at US$1,565. A fully loaded version with color graphics carried a price tag of US$6,000. Options offered included *PC-DOS*

9 Wikipedia, www.wikipedia.org, March 2007

1.0 (Microsoft's *MS-DOS*), *Microsoft BASIC*, *VisiCalc*, *UCSD Pascal*, *CP/M-86*, and *Easywriter* 1.0. IBM initially sold the new computer to consumers through Sears, Roebuck & Co. and ComputerLand.

I still have PC #6 in storage. Units #1 through #5 were test units that never left the Boca facility. On announcement day, I had already moved to Rochester, Minnesota, to assume a different role within IBM. The Boca group sent a contingent to Rochester to present me with the first commercial unit off the line. It was a proud moment for me, to see this actually come to fruition.

No More Dancing Lessons

But in the midst of all of this excitement, not too long after the project had been approved, the General Manager of IBM's Rochester, Minnesota, operation, Hal Martin, unexpectedly passed away. I got a call from Frank Carey, who said, "Bill, we would like you to take over the Rochester, Minnesota, facility. I know you want to stay in Boca, and you want to do the PC. But we will know if you are truly a 'good guy' if you take this position."

I had worked in low end and midrange systems for the previous 15 years. At any other time in my career, the move would have been a plum of a job. I had only been in Boca for two years; to go from Lab Director responsible for 1,300 developers to GM of a facility like Rochester was a huge leap. The Rochester facility was responsible for mid-range development and ultimately produced the very successful AS-400 mini-computer. The mid-range product line for which I became responsible was about a $25 billion business at that time and had millions of square feet in its plants; the General Manager in Rochester had lots of responsibility. I didn't want to leave Boca, Carey was right about that, but I felt that I was not given much choice.

Once again, *I*'d *B*een *M*oved. I left the Boca Raton project in the hands of Don Estridge who had been running the Series/1 program and packed my bags. And the elephant stopped going to his dancing lessons.

The Series/1 Story

When I went to Boca Raton in 1978, one of the projects I was responsible for was the Series/1, as well as a dot matrix printer and a lower end commercial product. But by far the biggest responsibility in Boca at that time was the Series/1. I also had my little project with three people to look at the micro opportunity.

Announced by IBM's General Systems Division (GSD) on November 16, 1976, the IBM Series/1 was a small, general purpose computing system offering both communications and sensor-based capabilities. It allowed users to attach a large number and variety of input and output devices, including custom-built devices for special application requirements.

Initially provided in two versions — the Model 3 (IBM 4953) and the Model 5 (IBM 4955) — the Series/1 was offered at prices ranging from $10,000 to $100,000 depending upon configuration. The first Series/1 machines were delivered to Citibank N.A. in New York City and to Quaker City Motor Parts in Middletown, Delaware, under a test marketing program begun in April 1976.[10] A version of Series/1 was used as an agency-level computer at State Farm Insurance. The Series/1 competed with other minicomputers of the time, including the PDP-11 from Digital Equipment Corporation (DEC) and offerings from Data General and HP.

But the Series/1 had never worked well. It was plagued with software problems from the moment it was introduced. No one could figure out why; we had high quality people on the project with the software operation headed up by Philip "Don" Estridge. As I looked into the situation, I learned that Don had made an agreement with the sales and marketing organization that when he shipped the product, his job was over. He maintained that the product worked, and that if any problems occurred after it was shipped and installed, the field was committed to fix those problems. But the field didn't have the ability to fix the problems. These problems were severe enough that they could only be addressed by the development group.

Once I discovered this, I called Don in and said, "You have to fix these problems."

He said, "No. I have an agreement with the field that it is not my responsibility."

I said, "But Don, you are the only one that can fix the problems." He insisted on sticking to his agreement, so I said, "Well, then, you are out of a job."

I reassigned Don, brought in a new program manager. In the two intervening years, we fixed the software problems and the Series/1 started going well. The biggest Series/1 installation was the State Farm agent system, where we deployed something like 14,000 units. Ultimately, Don came back to me asking if I would entrust him to manage the State Farm project; I agreed. He did a fabulous job. It was a great project that worked, was delivered on time, and made money.

After the project was completed when Don learned that I would be leaving for Rochester, Minnesota, he came to me and asked if I would entrust him with the PC program and leadership of the Boca operation. He was a very bright guy with charismatic leadership qualities, and he understood software. I knew that software would be the key to the PC's success. Don believed in the project and understood the business principles (including the Life Boat Rule). I put him in place to run the operation when I left.

The Rest of the Story

By transferring me out of the program, IBM made one of the classic mistakes identified by Harvard's Kantor:[11] She uses Honeywell as an example but could just as easily have used Boca Raton, saying:

Changes in team composition that result from companies' preferences for the frequency with which individuals make career moves can make it hard for new ventures to deal with difficult challenges, prompting them to settle for quick, easy, conventional solutions. At Honeywell in the 1980s, leaders of new-venture teams were often promoted out of them before the work had been completed. Because promotions were take-it-or-leave-it offers and pay was tied to size of assets controlled (small by definition in new ventures) rather than difficulty of task, even dedicated innovators saw the virtues of leaving their projects midstream. Honeywell was undermining its own innovation efforts. An executive review of why new ventures failed uncovered this problem, but a technology bias made it hard for old-school managers of that era to increase their appreciation for the value of team bonding and continuity.

---

11 *Innovation: The Classic Traps,* by Rosabeth Moss Kantor, Harvard Business Review, November 2006

My transfer to Rochester was the beginning of IBM's slide back to "business as usual" and its squelching of the budding Pragmatic Innovation process I had set in motion. But there were several other contributing factors that I will discuss in some detail. From my perspective in Rochester and later, in White Plains before I took over the top technology job for half of IBM, I watched as Don managed the PC program and eventually observed how IBM began to pull it back in to the mainstream organization, abandoning the principles of Pragmatic Innovation and the Life Boat Rule. These are some of my observations.

It wasn't long before Don Estridge reverted to form. Part of my initial proposal was that three years after launch, there would be second generation PC. This was based on what we—and our outside consultants and associates—saw as the next need, based on Moore's Law relative to the inverse ratio of the increase in processing power and the reduction in price of technology. We believed that ultimately, users would want to be able to take advantage of increased processing power, memory, storage, and more. That aspect of the plan received no focus under Don's leadership. Instead, Don came up with a home PC, which was ultimately brought to market as the PC Junior, an arbitrarily reduced function computer for the home. The product failed, leaving significant finished goods inventory issues behind it. From a hardware perspective, the PC program was going in exactly the wrong direction, and there was no second generation plan in place.

From a software perspective, Don kept the program on track. Our plan was to become number one, and we got to that position quickly because of the open architecture. We shipped more applications than Apple, who was our chief competitor at the time. Apple didn't have an open architecture. We had all the players writing applications for us; ultimately, the real value they got was in being able to write not only for the IBM PC, but for the clone PCs as well. The market was bigger than anyone ever anticipated; and many of the household names in the software industry, including Microsoft, got their start by developing applications for the IBM PC.

In early 1985, I was asked to become President of the Entry Systems Division to replace Don Estridge. I found that in my absence, he had made several mistakes which were reminiscent of his Series/1 experience. He had taken to heart several decisions I had made when we set up the project and would not change them, even though the business had grown and needed more sophisticated organizational treatment. The most serious of these was allowing every development group to operate independently without an overriding architecture to guide the work.

I said, "Don, why do you have eight life boats all doing their own thing? You now have a complex system, and you have no architecture. There are no rules that identify, for example, how the communications function interacts with the file management function. The stuff doesn't work."

His answer? "Well, you told me the best way to do this business was in a life boat."

I said, "But now the business has changed, and you haven't changed with it."

By moving me out of the program, the company made a critical mistake. I believe I had the experience, the passion, and the desire to make that transition, but they did not even recognize the need for a transition. What I saw that apparently others did not was the need to keep innovating. I understood that this market was changing rapidly, and we had to change with it or ahead of it. The strong IBM culture lulled others into a false sense of security and superiority; as a result, the innovative spirit we had developed in Boca was gone.

I was able to fix most of the problems when I returned, although we lost a lot of time doing it. Among others, we had the PC Junior debacle; the release of the PC/XT with a disk drive from a third party vendor that didn't work; the ignoring of the second generation PC, which still had not launched by 1985; and the fact that under Estridge's leadership, IBM had not developed an architecture for the PC to control the growing number of competing functions like the hard disk and communications.

Sadly, Don and his wife, Mary Ann, along with nine other IBM employees from Boca, died in a Delta Airlines crash shortly after I replaced him in Boca. He had been well liked by the people there, and his death had a big impact on morale. We had a week with eleven funerals in Boca Raton for Boca employees and family members — the flight from Ft. Lauderdale to Dallas was used by our people on the way to our other location in Austin. It was a tragic time.

The Wizard of OS

When we committed to bringing a PC to market in a year, the logic was that we could not do it in a year if we had to create our own operating system (OS). We never would have been able to navigate the IBM bureaucracy in time. Some of my team, including Jack Sams, had already looked at the software available in the marketplace. He thought Kildall's CP/M would be the way to go. Between the time we had the first meeting with the Corporate Management Committee and the time we had arranged to present our plan, we only had two weeks. Those trips to the West Coast to see Gates and Kildall were critical, and Gates' ultimate agreement to work with us on the operating system was a key element of the ultimate success of the program.

Talk about no-nonsense Pragmatic Innovation: Bill Gates and the early history of Microsoft epitomized this philosophy, although Microsoft itself ultimately fell into many of the classic innovation traps as it grew bigger. It was very clear that Bill Gates and Steve Ballmer saw working with IBM as a huge opportunity; it was unfortunate that Gary Kildall did not feel the same. Nonetheless, we were really sticking our necks out by partnering with this unproven company. When we went to the second Corporate Management Committee meeting, although we had identified the operating system we had never tested it or seen any documentation on it. It wasn't until a week or two after that second meeting that Gates and Ballmer visited White Plains to flesh out the plan and began to put a development schedule in place. At that point in time, we were on such a fast track from an IBM point of view that we weren't focusing on how things would be done; we were just getting them done. But in a departure from IBM protocol, I had obtained a commitment from IBM management that the operating system would remain under Microsoft ownership, with IBM simply licensing it.

Gates was smart, and that was an exciting time in technology. Bill Gates, Steve Jobs, and SUN's Scott McNealy were all really bright; it was a pleasure to work with them over the years. I learned a great deal from the way they did business. Much later, I negotiated acquisition of Steve Jobs' NeXTSTEP operating system (after he departed Apple and founded his new company, NeXT) to use with the IBM System/7. I remember at that time that I had 13,000 development people in my division at IBM, and Steve had 120. After I got to meet them, I thought 20 of them were world class. Out of my 13,000, I probably could identify six world class developers. Do the math. These early computing visionaries attracted great people and really did wonderful things without large company constraints. By that time, IBM had almost completely reverted to form, and any remaining Pragmatic Innovation influences were dissipating.

On the bigger picture IBM side, there were a whole series of things that happened to push us further back into the old ways. By 1982, Opel was CEO and Chairman; Kuehler was President and Krowe was CFO. They decided they were going to take IBM from a $65 billion company to a $120 billion company, which, by the way, they never achieved. In order to generate cash, over a three-year period they sold off IBM leases, which had been providing significant annuity revenue. Those sales generated cash and several years of such high performance and profit that they looked like heroes. But in 1985 there was an economic turndown; for the first time IBM laid people off and closed plants because management had sold off the annuity. At that same time, people began to realize that the little PC was using more logic and memory technology than the rest of IBM put together, and it was all being acquired outside.

Kuehler forced us to start using inside sources for technology. That meant that the whole precept upon which the program was built was thrown out the door. In fairness to Kuehler, the original idea was that we would have a mechanism for determining outside prices to force inside prices to match. But the inside technology guys couldn't even come close to matching outside costs, because they were burdened with IBM processes and financial ratios. Kuehler did, of course, discourage our pointing that fact out to Armonk. Gone was the Life Boat Rule. The program was forced to use internal technology anyway, causing a serious market disadvantage for the PC. The elephant could now put that dance card in a museum, because it created one of the most deadly innovation traps that Kantor identifies: "Tight controls strangle innovation."

Another major blow to the program was its sales strategy shift. Originally, we were selling solely through external channels, but when the PC became so popular, the IBM internal sales force demanded the right to sell PCs to large accounts with the idea being that they would own the large accounts and give the stores the small ones. It should have been obvious to everyone that the large accounts were the stores' largest opportunity as well; this move created a humungous channel problem. We had two major channels—the stores and the direct sales force—bidding the PC's price down. In fact, PCs were often "thrown into the deal for free" by the direct sales force when it could make the difference on a mainframe sale.

The Final Blow

The final blow was the decision to build the Systems Application Architecture (SAA). In large accounts, the sales force had tried to position IBM as the sole partner a company needed, because now that they had PCs in their bag, IBM could meet all of a company's computing needs. However, customers would respond that, although IBM could meet all of their needs, the product lines were not compatible with each other. It was almost as hard to make IBM's products work together as it was to make their products work with other people's.

To address that issue, IBM developed what it called Systems Application Architecture, or SAA. Earl Wheeler was the top programming guy at IBM at the time and came up with the Systems Application Architecture. He had a close working partnership with Jack Kuehler. This architecture was designed to provide a consistent user interface for IBM's broad computing platform by putting a second generation PC in front of every piece of IBM hardware. This would overcome the difficulty of using different interfaces for different models and families of computers that customers were complaining about, as well as to make it easier to integrate disparate IBM products. To do that, he had to emulate all of the old displays, including the 3270 families. In other words, those PC's needed extra software that would allow them to connect to those disparate systems. As part of that project, IBM had an agreement with Gates that we would share 50/50 ownership of the second-generation operating system, which would be called OS/2. In deference to that agreement, Gates abandoned his planned development of what ultimately became Windows.

Adding that emulation software to OS/2 added a significant burden to the operating system; it required much more programming and more memory and disk space to operate. At one point, there were over 11,000 programmers around the world working on this problem, about 100 of which were from Microsoft. The Microsoft people, comprising less than one percent of the programming force, were doing most of the work aimed at improving the individual productivity of PC users. The rest of the programming staff was focused on meeting the needs demanded by the Systems Application Architecture. Although this drove Gates nuts, he stuck with the program.

One day I got a call from Bill. He said, "What the heck are you doing?" Kuehler had announced a deal with DEC, agreeing that the two companies would put together a consortium, the Open Software Foundation (OSF), to build a universal UNIX for everyone in the world to use. UNIX was the other major issue IBM customers had with the company. We had stuck with DOS and OS, which were closed, proprietary systems, while most of our competitors offered some version of UNIX. Base UNIX could was available for limited or no cost, and its language and architecture were well documented in the public domain. This meant that it was easy for third parties to write applications based on the operating system. It also reduced the software licensing costs the manufacturer had to pass on to customers. In mixed shops, which were becoming increasingly common, customers wanted IBM to have a UNIX offering to more easily integrate into the enterprise computing environment. That was part of the reason I later negotiated with Jobs to acquire the right to use NeXTSTEP, a UNIX-based operating system. IBM talked a good story but never really did anything meaningful with UNIX. It seems that the DEC announcement was more of the same.

I called Jack Kuehler and said, "I think we have just lost Gates."

Jack said, "Well, you know we are never going to build that UNIX system. It was only posturing."

I said, "Do you want me to call Gates and tell him that the President of IBM was lying?"

"No," he said, "but I expect you to handle it."

In the end, I think Gates really wanted to do Windows. He had put the project on hold in respect of his OS/2 arrangement with IBM, but this gave him the excuse to move forward with it. He was angry and very frustrated after all those years of working with IBM.

Much later, in 1990, when I was CEO of Gulfstream, we picked Bill up in Nebraska, where he had gone to a football game between the University of Washington and the University of Nebraska with Warren Buffett. My wife, Cristina, and I stopped there with our Gulfstream GIV jet to fly Bill out to Laguna Niguel, California, where we were both recognized with awards for the best software and hardware of the last decade. On the way out, we talked over these old issues. Bill said, "I thought it was hard dealing with IBM when you were there, but after you left it became impossible."

Grinding the Bones of the PC Business

Although there were many good things about IBM, there were many things I found frustrating as well. When I was at the Entry Systems Division (ESD), which included the PC business, I had responsibility for Boca Raton, Raleigh, Austin, and some overseas locations. In Austin, we were developing a new engineering workstation system using the RISC architecture, to be launched as System/7. We needed a UNIX operating system for it. I negotiated with Steve Jobs, who had left Apple to found NeXT, to license his UNIX operating system, NeXTSTEP. Ross Perot was an investor in NeXT. I used to meet with Steve at Ross's office in Dallas. You could not help but be impressed with Steve and his people at NeXT. We spent $80 million to license that system, which was, of course, approved by IBM management.

Ultimately, we didn't use it because Jack Kuehler didn't want to have a better UNIX operating system at the low end of the line than they did in their high-end systems. Additionally, my relationship with Kuehler had continued to deteriorate, and I found that he was trying to block much that I did. NeXTSTEP and IBM's UNIX strategy was another casualty of his political approach to business ventures.

This situation brought my experience with Pragmatic Innovation at IBM full circle. I had gone through the exhilarating period of building the PC with the support of Frank Carey, where I first began to develop my philosophy of Pragmatic Innovation and prove that it worked. We had limited support from Kuehler and Opel, of course. After Carey left, these men, along with Krowe, began to wreak havoc with the PC business and with the company as a whole by selling off the leased inventory. That created huge financial pressures, and, in response to that pressure, they ground the bones of the PC business to shore up the rest of the company. By 1988, the business was exhausted.

DINNER WITH STEVE

When we were negotiating the NeXTSTEP deal with Steve Jobs, Steve arranged a dinner at his house with our software and legal people. I was probably the youngest IBM person there, and I was over 40. Steve, at the time, was in his late 20s. All of the IBM people wore blue suits, white shirts, and ties and were seated on one side of the table. All of the NeXT kids on the other side of the table wore whatever they felt like—and I can guarantee you that none of them had chosen a suit and tie. Steve's house had essentially no furniture. He had a big BMW motorcycle in the living room, which was his baby and reminded him of his youth.

He served us pasta with chunks of tomatoes and fresh flowers on top. Looking around that table, I thought, "This is the most amazing thing I have ever seen. Here we are, five years after the famous Apple Superbowl Lemmings commercial, in Steve Jobs' house with IBM in blue suits on one side and his guys on the other. How ironic. Some things never change."

IBM's Comeback

John Akers, Chairman and CEO after Opel[12], had to clean up the mess he had inherited from Opel, Krowe and Kuehler, and it did him in. I remember when he recommended layoffs for the first time. Carey, Watson, and Opel, three former Chairmen, were on his Board at the time, and they all exclaimed that they never had to lay people off. But in reality the decisions they had made in selling off of leased inventory caused the problem that Akers was now facing. IBM eventually brought in Lou Gerstner, who changed the whole balance of the company by bringing in the services business, which led to IBM's comeback. The focus then shifted to services, and IBM divested itself of all of its nonmainframe hardware businesses, including the PC. In early 2007, it finally converted its Printing Systems Division, InfoPrint Solutions Company, into a joint venture between IBM and Ricoh. From a financial perspective, IBM did a marvelous job of restructuring its business, but only time will tell if there is sufficient momentum in place to keep it going.

Lessons Learned

One of the most important lessons I learned during my IBM experience is that when it comes to innovation, it is critical to have the support of an

---

12 According to IBM archives, Akers became CEO in February of 1985 and assume the additional role of Chairman in June 1986.

executive at the top of the organization that is willing to think out of the box. Frank Carey was just such an executive, and IBM didn't have another of that caliber until Lou Gerstner arrived.

The way the PC came to market was very unique from an IBM perspective. For a new business like that, you have to be creative in thinking about how best to operate the business to make it successful. While it may have all or some elements of the business operations of your (previously successful) base business, it is very likely that many of those elements won't work in a new business. You have to consciously make decisions across the board, even down to items like changing internal and external terms and conditions, and in doing so, understand both the rewards and penalties.

In the case of the IBM PC, you couldn't have the people who were responsible for the high end business (the old world) involved. It is like entering a new war with a nuclear submarine where everyone else is driving a battleship or an aircraft carrier. New wars require new approaches and different tools. I had control of the nuclear sub in Boca, and they put me back on a battleship in Rochester, Minnesota.

Not even Microsoft is immune to the classic innovation traps. As much respect as I have for Bill Gates, I truly believe that had he split the company into two or three pieces, all reporting to the same holding company, he would have avoided a lot of the grief of his now-famous run-ins with the DOJ, and he would have increased shareholder value. Just like in the old IBM days, the efforts Microsoft is making to enter new businesses and address new areas of opportunity are being metered, corralled, and contained because of the requirement to continue to feed the beast that got them there in the first place. It appears to me that Microsoft's most recent operating system, Vista, has similar problems to those we encountered with OS/2. Microsoft Vista is another example of protecting a battleship, this time while under attack by new nuclear submarines such as Google.

Later in this book, I will talk specifically about how an organization can apply the principles of Pragmatic Innovation to not only launch new businesses but almost more importantly, build a sustaining culture that will foster innovation far into the future. I will also provide insight and guidance on how to help members of the "old" business transition to the "new" businesses and contribute to the overall organizational innovation.

New Opportunities

I changed the way IBM did business by putting the Boca group together and looking outside of IBM at the way Apple and other companies worked, the way people were collaborating on hardware and software technology, and how they were using new and different sales and marketing channels. It was very unusual for an IBM project at that time to have a group of people who were, instead of drinking our own bathwater, going out to find out what bathwater other people were drinking. We had to change our T's and C's and our internal development cycle to get the program down to a year yet not give up quality. It was a fascinating process of gathering information and finding data that we didn't have before, doing competitive analyses, and putting together a business plan with the right processes in place to be successful in a new market.

While the original Pragmatic Innovation approach allowed IBM to move out of its standard processes to "teach the elephant to dance," eventually IBM pulled the innovative activities back into the mainstream and stifled them by:

- Forcing the use of internal sales and service, disenfranchising a successful external sales channel

- Implementing poor cash management practices which created financial pressures and reduced business flexibility

- Mandating the PC business to use internal technology at a price disadvantage

- Adding too much overhead to OS/2 in an attempt to solve large account system architecture issues on other products that had nothing to do with the PC (i.e., adding the requirement to emulate all of IBM's other front-end systems, such as the 3270)

- Ruining the Microsoft relationship through its posturing with DEC on OSF

- And finally, closing Boca due to cash and management issues driven by the leasing portfolio sell-off.

When the PS/2, the second generation PC, finally got to market, IBM's share of sales in the dealers' inventory had slipped from 80 percent to about 30 percent.

For me, IBM had become much less fun. The PC business was under a lot of pressure because of the litany of mistakes noted above, and we were no longer profitable. In my last year at IBM, I remember that Rod Canion shipped 150,000 PCs from Compaq and received a $3 million bonus. I shipped a million and a half PCs and got a $30,000 bonus. That is about the time I decided to get involved with something I thought would be more entrepreneurial, as we will see in Chapter Three.

CHAPTER 3

More Than a Copy

"The secret of success in life is
for a man to be ready for his opportunity when it comes."

BENJAMIN DISRAELI (1804-1881)

Xerox is well known for both its successes and failures in the marketplace. The company invented and brought to market dry-toner electrophotography, which it dubbed xerography, in 1959. At the time, the company was called Haloid Xerox. Its first product was the Xerox 914, so named because it could reproduce documents up to 9" x 14" in size. Xerox dominated that market and grew to $8.5 billion in revenues by 1983. But by the mid-1970s, Japanese manufacturer Savin was nipping at the heels of the photocopier giant, followed by other Japanese competitors who were leveraging innovation to compete with Xerox' aging product line. Where once Xerox literally owned the copier market, by 1982, the company had less than 40 percent market share.[1] Sounds a lot like the IBM PC Story ...

The Xerox 914 had a price tag way in excess of any of its existing competition at the time—$29,500 compared to $400 for a wet process copier. Xerox took a page out of IBM's book by establishing a leasing program that allowed customers to lease the copier for $95 per month, which included 2,000 free copies and five cents a copy beyond that. People thought no one would ever make that many copies per month, but Xerox' rapid growth belied that assumption. Also like IBM, Xerox seriously underestimated not only the number of copies that would be made, but the overall market demand for this new device. In the first six months, more Xerox 914 units were sold than the entire estimated lifetime demand for the product, and the company could have sold more had they had more manufacturing capacity. The 914 took about 15 seconds to make the first copy, and then cranked them out at seven copies a minute after that.

Xerox leveraged the leasing model into a huge cash cow, ultimately establishing its own captive leasing business, which was only recently offloaded to GE Capital.

In an article published at Xerox' 25th anniversary, Murray Rothbard of the Ludwig von Mises Institute, a think tank located

---

1 *Making Economic Sense*, by Murray Rothbard, The Ludwig von Mises Institute. Chapter 54, Competition at Work: Xerox at 25.

in, of all places, Eastern Alabama, quoted Horace Becker, Chief Engineer for the 914, as saying, ""Technically, it did not look like a winner . . . That which we did, a big company could not have afforded to do. We really shot the dice, because it didn't make any difference." Haloid Xerox spent some $20 million and 12 years developing the product. According to Xerox lore, more than 20 companies, including Eastman Kodak and IBM, were offered the opportunity to develop the electrophotographic copier, but all turned it down, saying it was too complex, too costly and would only have a small market.

Meanwhile, as the 1970s came to a close, Xerox realized it had serious quality issues that were affecting its ability to continue to dominate the market it had invented. Japanese competitors were able to sell copiers for less than it cost Xerox to manufacture its units, and they were often more functional. The quality problems at Xerox resulted in severe reliability issues for its products, in addition to an excessive cost of manufacturing.

Then-Chairman David Kearns initially worked with Tony Kobayashi, son of the CEO of Fuji Photo and a joint venture partner with Xerox in Fuji Xerox, to learn about the quality movement in Japan that was at least partially responsible for the growing Japanese dominance in the copier market. Fuji Xerox had won the Deming Prize in 1980, Japan's highest award for quality,[2] and Kearns wanted to know more.

Kearns jumped on the emerging Total Quality Management (TQM) bandwagon with great gusto, one of the earliest U.S. companies to do so, engaging Dr. Edwards Deming, who was known as the father of the Japanese post-war industry revival and often thought of as the leading quality guru in

---

2   Xerox Factbook

the United States. Kearns and his executive team began leveraging quality principles to improve manufacturing and began to develop a TQM process for Xerox. Called Leadership Through Quality, it would reenergize and reinvent the company. The program was announced in 1983. With its quality work underway in the background, by 1982 Xerox had begun to make a comeback with its highly successful 10-Series copiers, the industry's first to use built-in microcomputers with a low-bandwidth Ethernet network as the internal communications interface.[3]

Largely due to its quality initiatives and Kearns' strong leadership, Xerox was successful in reducing the cost of manufacturing, improving product quality and innovation, and grabbing back market share from the Japanese manufacturers.

Systemic Change

David Kearns drove another initiative along with Leadership Through Quality. He and Paul Allaire, then President, decided to begin hiring people throughout the organization—but particularly in senior management—who had a systems background. He believed this influx of people with a different mental model from the conventional copier sales people would stimulate new growth strategies for the company. He realized that Xerox:

- had not effectively capitalized on the innovation taking place at its world-class Palo Alto Research Center (PARC);

- managers and executives were running with the same copier-style sales plays in a world that was rapidly changing, because that was what they had been successful with in the past;

- growth appeared to be stalled due to a lack of strategic vision that would not be cured by the quality movement.

Among the high-level executives that joined the company during this phase in its life included:

- John Lopiano, an experienced systems development manager from IBM who headed up the company's high-speed printing systems business, and whose primary competitive target was IBM

- Len Vickers, an experienced marketing executive who hailed from GE and headed a newly formed centralized marketing organization

- Barbara Pellow, a successful IBM sales and marketing professional brought in to manage market development for what ultimately turned out to be a flagship product for the company in the 1990's, the DocuTech Production Publisher

- Tom Maletta, an experienced systems finance professional from IBM who was tasked with refitting stagnant Xerox financial policies.

It was in that period that I left IBM to join Xerox as the Executive Vice President of Worldwide Development and Manufacturing.

Kearns hoped that by infusing a new systems culture with experienced leadership from outside the company into the existing Xerox culture, he would be able to blend this new blood with current systems literate employees in order to develop new business strategies and stimulate growth for the company.

In fact, this not only resulted in new product development and marketing strategies that would set the company on a path to renewed growth, but it also resulted in the adoption of new business practices based on an understanding of how the world was evolving and progressing outside the company. It set the stage for recapturing the energy and excitement that was Xerox in its heyday, channeling that energy into the development of a company that was more aligned with the future.

Hiring these leaders from outside the company naturally led to more external hiring, as each of us brought in more new blood throughout our organizations. For example, I hired Al Dugan from GE to head up Manufacturing; he became part of a very effective team that included long-time Xeroids Chip Holt, Brian Stern, Sandy Campbell, and Ron Rider from PARC.

This influx of new ways of thinking and behaving at Xerox set the stage for the second implementation of Pragmatic Innovation in my career.

A Big Decision

Although I had made the decision to move on from IBM for reasons I have already laid out, I was not sure which direction to go. I was interviewing with both telecom giant AT&T and Xerox as I thought about what to do next.

I had been with IBM for 26 years and had moved 17 times. My kids were in high school in Chappaqua, New York, and neither the kids nor my wife at the time wanted to relocate yet again. With AT&T, I would have had to relocate to New Jersey. The Xerox job was an easy commute from Chappaqua to Stamford.

Loyalty to IBM was also a factor in choosing Xerox. With AT&T's recent acquisition of computing firm NCR and the creation of a computing division, AT&T was shaping up to be a significant IBM competitor. I believed that IBM would be more comfortable with the Xerox choice than with an AT&T choice for competitive reasons.

Finally, it was a great opportunity, reporting directly to Paul Allaire as Executive Vice President of Worldwide Development and Manufacturing for the company.

During the interview process, I did have one heart-stopping experience. I was heading to Boston to speak at an industry trade show and had arranged to meet an AT&T representative at the private jet terminal at Boston's Logan Airport for another interview. As I was heading out, I received a call from IBM Chairman John Akers, who said, "Bill, I have just been invited to play in a golf game at Baltusrol with AT&T CEO Bob Allen and their head of service. I would like you to join us." Well, that was an interesting turn of events! When I mentioned it to my Boston AT&T contacts, it threw them into a tizzy. They were adamant that I could not let Akers know I was interviewing with Allen. Of course, I would not have done that anyway, but it did create quite a stir. It was a good golf game, by the way. Allen and I were partners, and Akers teamed with the other AT&T executive. I ended up parring three of the last four holes, and Allen and I won. Nothing ever leaked out about the employment discussions, but Allen was so happy to have beaten the IBM Chairman that he ran into the golf shop and bought me a shirt.

Following the game, the AT&T folks told me that Allen had really enjoyed the day and wanted me to join AT&T. It made the decision harder, but I ultimately did choose Xerox.

The Two Faces of Xerox

But by that time, the monolithic firm had slumped back into innovation gridlock. Once incredibly innovative and starting to make a comeback from its near-death experience with Japanese competition primarily as a result of the quality movement, the pendulum swung too far, as pendulums will do. While the Leadership Through Quality movement initially energized the company, it ultimately mired Xerox in even greater bureaucracy. In 1988, when I joined Xerox, the Quality movement was well-entrenched in the company. Xerox would win the esteemed Malcolm Baldridge National Quality Award in 1989, a testament to the people and leadership of a company which came back from the brink of disaster to once again assume a leadership role in the copier market.

But with the pendulum swing, it seemed that every step of the quality process needed to be checked off in almost every decision made across the then-100,000-employee company before a decision could be made! Any organization within Xerox that had more than 30 employees had its own Quality Executive—the Quality Police—to make sure the process was followed down to the tiniest detail. At IBM, any organization of any size, especially after the Consent Decree, had a legal department, or at least a lawyer, assigned to it. As you might imagine, that consumed a lot of management time. But it was nothing compared to the Quality process as it bloomed into full bureaucratic flower at Xerox.

I still remember the first meeting I went to at Xerox. It was a meeting about the high-end printer business, and we got into a discussion about a strategy for displacing IBM's high end printers. Having just come from IBM, that was a subject that I understood very well. I started to propose an action plan for implementing the project they had identified. Our quality representative stopped me and said, "You are processing. This is an information sharing meeting and you are not supposed to process solutions." I said, "I know the answer to this one, so I am simply going to skip the next meeting and answer the question now." Although that is exactly what we did, it did not get me off to a good start with the Xerox Quality Police.

Also of great interest to me was the other, less well known side of Xerox that Kearns and Allaire were trying to bolster with the rash of outside hires—

its computer-related businesses, and most particularly, the Palo Alto Research Center (PARC). I was anxious to understand why—after inventing the PC, the fax, the laser printer, networking, the software that was the foundation for Adobe, and more—Xerox had not taken advantage of any of these innovations. It was one of the first areas I looked at.

Copiers were the lifeblood of the company and clearly drove the business decisions, but Xerox had also invested heavily in research and development, not all of which was directly related to its core copier business. There were four research centers—the Xerox Research Centre of Canada, near Toronto, focused on materials research for things like toner; the Wilson Center for Research and Technology in Webster, New York, focused on systems integration and product-oriented research; the Xerox Research Centre of Europe, located in Grenoble, France, and focused on document-related research; and of course, the legendary Palo Alto Research Center (PARC) located in the heart of California's Silicon Valley.

PARC is known for developing the graphical user interface, drop down menus, computer networking, printer page description languages, laser printing, and a myriad of innovations that Xerox, for the most part, failed to effectively bring to market.[4] In each and every case, the company missed the opportunity to dominate those markets in the same way it had dominated the copier market in the early days. In fact, in his book, *Open Innovation*, Chesbrough documents no less than 24 Xerox PARC spin-off companies between 1979 and 1998, some of which were licensed Xerox spin-offs, but many of which were founded by frustrated Xerox escapees using venture capital funding. These included Robert Metcalfe's 3Com (1984—computer

---

4   It should be noted that the mouse, pull-down menu and graphical user interface were actually *invented* by Doug Englebart at Stanford Research Institute (SRI), but first *commercialized* by Xerox. Englebart rarely gets the credit he is due in literature discussing this period in history.

networking); John Warnock's Adobe (1983—software); Jack Balletto's VLSI (1983—integrated circuits), Tony Domit's Documentum (1990—document management); and Henry Sang's Computers and Technology, Inc. (1994—software and consulting).

"The Valley," as the technology cognoscenti referred to it, was heavily populated with ex-Xeroids in a wide range of technology companies, including one of the inventors of high-speed laser printing, Gary Starkweather, who defected to Apple Computer in 1987 after becoming disenchanted with Xerox' lack of strategy for and attention to color printing.

Xerox had tons of innovation within the organization, but in key areas, the company missed the boat on both protection of its intellectual property and the commercialization of its innovations. Xerox also suffered from a grand "not invented here" syndrome, and in fact, resisted working with other companies in a time when leading companies were beginning to reach out to accommodate a changing marketplace, like we did at IBM, at least with the PC program. Xerox failed to see the difference between standalone, analog copiers and networked computing and printing devices, in this regard. Top executives did not have the Frank-Carey-like vision required to rapidly adjust to a new, connected world. While Xerox actually invented a lot of what are today's standards, or the forebears thereof, the company insisted on working in a proprietary world.

The Xerox Alto was developed at Xerox PARC in 1973. It was an early minicomputer and the first computer to use the graphical user interface and a "desktop" metaphor. A number of applications were written for the Alto, including Bravo, an early word processing program that is remarkably similar to what was ultimately brought to market as Microsoft Word. The first real Xerox commercialization of this innovation was called the Star, a chunky workstation that could have up to a 40-Megabyte hard drive and could be attached to a network with a 30-page-per-minute laser printer. One workstation, one server, and one printer, the basic configuration, sold for about $100,000. It included a highly featured, integrated working environment, a lá today's Microsoft Windows and Microsoft Office combined, and was popular in government installations and the publications groups of large companies.

What I found upon investigation was that even though Xerox' developments were way ahead of what we had done at IBM in terms of functionality, the company had chosen to bring these products to market in a totally closed environment, from its operating system to its dedicated Xerox sales and service force. As a result, it was over-featured and overpriced. It was, in fact, exactly what IBM would have done had we not employed the principles of Pragmatic Innovation.

Although Xerox released a lighter-weight, less expensive version, the Xerox 6085, in the mid-1980's, it was too little too late for the company's meaningful participation in the world of digital desktops. The IBM PC had set the standard in price and functionality, and the closed architecture of products like the Xerox Star and the 6085 were on their way out. In a sideways recognition of the importance of the IBM PC, the 6085 even had a PC emulation feature that allowed you to—somewhat clumsily—run PC applications!

Sadly, the capability and stability of the workstation's ViewPoint software outshone Microsoft and Apple by miles, but it was not modular, and few users required all of its bells and whistles.

Thus buyers were increasingly reluctant to invest big dollars in heavy, proprietary systems that provided more than they would ever need or could ever take advantage of. Closed hardware and software interfaces discouraged third parties from enhancing the Xerox product. Xerox had quietly faded out of the workstation business by the mid-1990's.

On the laser printer side, even though Xerox invented the technology, the company focused on centralized or workgroup printers and missed the personal printer opportunity. Xerox woke up one day to find that revenues for HP's printer business exceeded the total revenues of Xerox! And HP didn't even make their own printer engines; they were sourced from Japanese manufacturer Canon.

A Closed Environment in an Open World

At the time I joined Xerox at the end of 1988, there were three primary businesses—copiers, workstations and giant laser printers primarily used in the data center environment. The company was just beginning to get into distributed laser printing and even color laser printing. The copier business received the lion's share of corporate attention and funding, and the "systems" businesses—laser printing and workstations—struggled to get its share of investments and the respect of their "toner-head[5]" peers at all levels of the organization, who were enjoying the bounty delivered by selling thousands of analog copiers and failed to see the relevance of their digital brethren.

---

5   A term used by the "systems" people inside Xerox to describe their copier counterparts, referring to their focus on putting marks on paper, or toner on paper. I remember seeing gray toner bottles dressed up like "Mr. Toner-head" in more than one Xerox systems sales cubicle as I made the rounds of the various sales offices.

The vast majority of executive positions were held by successful copier folk. Before the influx of systems-oriented outsiders such as myself, there was little systems expertise inside the company other than a few developers and the research whiz kids at PARC.

Who knew that these three markets would ultimately converge? I like to think that in some way, David Kearns saw it coming. There was Xerox, sitting on the leadership products and technology of the future. But the company needed a new understanding of the outside systems environment to pull it off.

Serendipitously for me, I joined Xerox at about the time that convergence began to occur. What an embarrassment of riches the company had in terms of intellectual property. And how embarrassing that it had failed to leverage those riches to the full extent of their potential. But all of that was about to change, big time.

All three businesses had been managed as separate silos, each having its own manufacturing, sales and marketing, and even service operations. When I assumed my new role, it was to bring these three seemingly disparate operations under one roof, so to speak, from a product development perspective. There were many synergies that could be leveraged across the three, but politics and turf wars often prevented cooperation among groups busy competing for R&D dollars and executive attention.

When I got to Xerox, I found a culture that had an interesting blend of energy and inertia. I thought IBM was bureaucratic, but at IBM John Akers developed a very effective meeting strategy when he managed the communications group. We had a rule that meetings were not to exceed one hour. That forced people to be prepared. At Xerox, I found that not only did executive meetings routinely last four hours, perhaps partly due to the influence of the Quality managers, but schedules were typically booked months in advance, making it necessary to book early, late or weekend meetings to deal with current issues. When those long-scheduled meetings finally took place, one would wonder how relevant the topics of discussion were at that point. Quite often, people outside of Xerox, including Wall Streeters, asked me to help them schedule meetings with Xerox executives because this scheduling habit made it extremely difficult to work with the company. Meetings were not particularly productive. There were pages and pages of pre-read which no one ever read, and unlike IBM, very little real staff work was done in advance of executive meetings. That's why they took four hours to hash everything out when, with good staff work and a modicum of preparation, hours of expensive executive time could have been applied more effectively.

One good process Xerox did have was a requirement that pre-reading material be provided at least 24 hours in advance of each meeting so that attendees could be better prepared. Unfortunately, I was receiving some four inches of pre-reading daily. That simply could not continue.

Taking on the Challenge

In my role at Xerox, I was responsible for about 26,000 of the company's 100,000+ employees, and about a billion dollars in discretionary development budget. I had 13 direct reports and was responsible for coordinating with the Xerox/Fuji joint venture in Japan, known as Fuji Xerox. It was a great experience, and I still have a lot of close friends from those Xerox days. Despite the company's many challenges, Xerox people as a whole are some of the nicest people I have worked with in my career. They are bright, dedicated and flexible. For the most part, they truly love the company and want it to succeed.

My 13 direct reports and I laid out our first year's budget in a three-hour meeting, rather than the four-month process that was the norm at Xerox. It was a wonderful way to get started, and it set the tone for my staff in terms of how they should be using their time—and mine.

One of the first things I did when I took over the reins was to establish a one-hour meeting rule and to require the meeting leader to prepare one page of pre-reading that everyone was responsible for digesting prior to the meeting. That way, people came to meetings prepared, and you could actually conduct business within that hour timeframe. Staff initially complained that it was too difficult to reduce meeting background and objectives down to one page. They were right—it was difficult. But this was one thing I had learned from John Akers at IBM—the work required to distill thoughts to one page really did make for more effective meetings and much more manageable schedules. It forced people to do staff work rather than leaving that work to be done in the meeting or having me do that work for them. In Akers' meetings, the first 40 minutes were used to present to him, and the last 20 were used to arrive at an appropriate decision. It was amazing how much work John got done and how many good decisions got made under his leadership. This process forced staff work to occur before the meetings, and it worked for me at Xerox as well.

I did find, though, that other executives in the company were unwilling to make similar changes in meetings they were responsible for, so unfortunately, I ended up sitting through too many of those four-hour, irrelevant sessions and still wading through way too much pre-read.

It wasn't the first—or the last—time in my career I was the Lone Ranger.

Putting Pragmatic Innovation to Work at Xerox

Apart from the great divide between Toner-heads and Systems people at Xerox, or maybe because of it, Xerox was a very closed environment. While IBM was beginning to head down the road to building an open architecture, Xerox was still very proprietary. I saw good opportunity to apply the principles of Pragmatic Innovation at Xerox, as well as to help streamline things along the way.

We quickly achieved some great results. In addition to shortening the average meeting duration in my organization, we shortened average development cycles for copiers and print engines from five years to three years by limiting the development of new paper management schemes. I found that engineers were spending an inordinate amount of time redesigning the paper path in copiers and printers—a 1950's technology. This prompted one Xerox executive to comment, "People have a tendency to focus in on the things they're most comfortable with and work them to death." I wanted them to spend time on the future, not the past. By requiring pre-approval prior to doing any paper path redesign, we not only shortened the average development cycle by two years, but we also freed up $200 million per year for new development. Amazing.

I also discovered that at Xerox, vendor costs were allowed to automatically increase at five to ten percent per year while others in the industry were putting pressure on vendors to reduce costs by that much annually. I brought Allan E. Dugan on board from GE, and he had a significant positive impact on reducing manufacturing costs and inventories. Al went on to become an Executive Vice President at Xerox.

Al informed our suppliers that we expected a minimum of 5 percent reduction in costs annually, in line with industry practices. Shortly thereafter, I was visited by a gentleman that I assumed represented the Mafia, who apparently controlled some of our suppliers. He expressed a hearty objection to this proposed new structure, suggesting that some Xerox executives could likely get hurt. I informed the gentleman that he was welcome to wait in my office while I engaged the FBI. He left, and I turned over the investigation to our lawyers and the FBI. Luckily for me, that was the last I heard of it, and our suppliers did begin to come in with the requisite price decreases.

In another discovery, I found that finished goods inventory at Xerox was equal to 24 percent of revenues. The industry standard was 8 percent to 10 percent, and we had over $1.4 billion in excess inventory. I learned that we were in this situation because Manufacturing routinely missed promised delivery schedules, and the field was stockpiling inventory in order to keep customers happy. While we were not able to correct the entire problem, we were able to take about $1 billion out of inventory and to improve the reliability of Manufacturing deliveries.

These accomplishments were things that were under my control in my new role and were just good management, in my opinion. Good management is a prerequisite to gaining the full benefits of Pragmatic Innovation. In an organization that is out of control, as this one was, you can innovate all you want, but it will be to no avail.

The DocuTech Story

Once I had the basics improving, I turned my attention to the bigger issue of Xerox' systems strategy. Xerox had proven it had plenty of innovation inside, but the majority of that innovation languished due to lack of attention or escaped to make money for others. At the time, Xerox was getting close to bringing to market perhaps its greatest innovation of all. Code-named Meridian, it was brought to market in October of 1990 as the Xerox DocuTech Production Publisher.

The DocuTech started out as the work of a small development project that was the brain child of Charles "Chip" Holt. Like the IBM PC, it almost didn't see the light of day. It was an amazing product that captured the attention of the marketplace in a big way and took advantage of a market convergence of copiers and computers. It was a bet-the-company venture that ultimately turned into a multi billion-dollar business for Xerox. It was a full ten years before there was a true competitor on the scene.[6] Even today, Xerox still benefits from a substantial DocuTech business.

Often characterized as a "print shop in a box," the initial DocuTech Production Publisher, with an entry price of a quarter of a million dollars, produced black & white 600 dot per inch (dpi) laser printing at an astonishing

---

6   The Digimaster 9110 was launched in 2000 as a result of a joint venture between German press manufacturer Heidelberg and the Eastman Kodak Company.

135 pages per minute while concurrently scanning paper documents. This was the first truly digital copier in the Xerox arsenal.

The existing analog copiers of the time, often referred to as "light lens" devices, used an electrophotographic process. The document to be copied is illuminated and passed over a lens (thus the term light lens), and its image is projected onto the drum or photoreceptor belt. Where light hits the drum (where there is no text or image), the electrostatic charge is released. The remaining charge is called a latent image and is a positive image of the original document. Toner is then applied to the drum and the particles are attracted to the latent image, creating a visible toner image, which is then transferred to a sheet of paper to which an opposing charge has been applied. In the analog, light lens world, the process starts all over again for the next copy, with the original being illuminated once again.

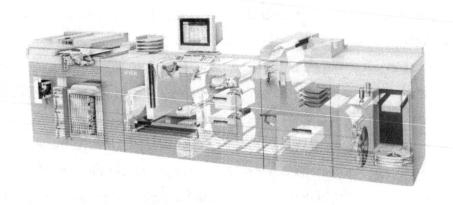

The Xerox DocuTech Production Publisher

In the digital world, originals are scanned once, and a laser is used to image the drum. During this digitizing process, an image of the page is scanned to a file that can be stored, manipulated, re-used, etc. This results in less wear and tear on originals being copied and provides some significant document processing benefits. One disadvantage to the analog copier model was its recirculating document mechanism which could recirculate originals to create collated sets. Although this was an important productivity enhancement to copying, it also was hard on originals which could be damaged, causing customer dissatisfaction. The document handler was often the weakest point of the copier. If it jammed, production was shut down and job recovery took time.

The concurrent operation designed into the DocuTech—i.e., the ability to simultaneously scan, print, and manipulate document images—was a critical differentiator for this digital technology about to foist itself into the world of analog printing. Printing from offset presses or analog copiers was a serial process; that is, a page is imaged and produced. Then the next page is imaged and produced, or in the case of copiers, the same page is imaged again when making multiple copies.

With the DocuTech, however, entire print jobs were scanned into a queue. Printing could begin as soon as the first scan was completed, and barring mechanical difficulties, the printer could continue to print from an infinite queue. The DocuTech's document handler was much gentler, only needing to handle each original once, with subsequent prints created from the electronic, scanned file. This was an increase in reliability, quality, and longevity of the originals—as well as an alleviator of customer dissatisfaction.

The DocuTech, from its touch screen interface, also allowed manipulation of scanned images. They could be cropped, rotated, and imposed into booklets. Pages from separate documents could be compiled into a single document, tabs could be added, images could be inserted—it truly was a "print shop in a box." It even had an inline tape binding system that could create bound books in line.

Prior to the DocuTech, all of these tasks were handled off-line, requiring multiple people and a great deal of time. Now the operations were all consolidated into one machine with one operator and concurrent processing that could handle scanning, document manipulation, and printing simultaneously. The productivity improvements were huge, and true print-on-demand was introduced to the world. In fact, it was not unusual to have one operator managing two or even three machines.

The DocuTech also had error recovery built in. So if there was a paper jam, or an error when producing a two-sided job, the DocuTech could recover itself, spitting out the seven pages already in the paper path, picking up the job where it left off with the error. This eliminated the need for a manual error recovery process that was wasteful and error prone, often resulting in the need to throw away hundreds of pages that were copied incorrectly or spending excessive time salvaging the "good" pages.

Although the first DocuTech couldn't accept digital input from a network or send digital information (like scanned images) back out, its on-board scanner and "scan once print many" model revolutionized the world of copying. This digital printing process—sometimes called electronic reprographics—is simple. A drum inside the press is electrostatically charged by a laser with the contents of a digital file; toner adhering to the charged (imaged) areas of the drum is transferred to paper or another substrate; and the toner then is fused to the paper with heat and pressure. That part of the process is similar to analog copying.

But unlike analog copying, the drum can be re-imaged from any designated page already scanned into the system. This means that documents can be electronically pre-collated, delivering book blocks or fully collated documents at the back end of the press. With offset printing, the other technology that DocuTech threatened to displace, new printing plates are required for each new page, and a separate collating process is required, extending the time and cost required to produce a printed job.

We will talk more about the impact the DocuTech had on the printing industry as a whole a bit later in this chapter.

Disruptive Change

As the product was being conceptualized and designed, Xerox realized that it had the potential to decimate its laser printer and light lens copier business. Kearns, according to Holt, wanted to make sure that Xerox was the first company that developed this product because he did not want to be facing it from a competitor.

But when I arrived on the scene, I realized that the DocuTech had much more potential than it was going to be able to deliver at launch. There did not seem to be a systems strategy backing up the product's future. Most particularly, Xerox did not have a concise color strategy, although color technology was being developed. In fact, Xerox was on its second or third generation of color products at that point and had not been particularly successful with color in the marketplace up to that point. The consensus, as a result of those failures, was that we were too far ahead of the market, and that there was no demand for color.

I recall being part of the decision when IBM started to build color displays for computers. A large faction at IBM thought no one would pay a premium for color. But once we did provide color displays, our biggest problem was meeting the market demand. I believed that the same would be true with copiers and/or printers that had the right feature set and price point. At Xerox, I put aggressive color development programs in place in both the copier and printer divisions with the help of John Lopiano, who had also just joined the company from IBM. We eventually executed those with a great deal of success.

In addition, Xerox had stuck to its proprietary model in terms of its product strategy. While the rest of the world had moved to PostScript as the *de facto* page description language and a TCP/IP communications protocols, the DocuTech was an Interpress[7] machine that internally used XNS[8], a Xerox proprietary communications protocol. This would make it difficult to integrate once it was connected to a network.

The lack of connectivity and the closed proprietary nature of the product would stunt its growth potential. We needed an open architecture that allowed us to take advantage of both front-end and back-end processes offered by other companies. We needed partners that could extend the DocuTech's functionality in the real-world environment of the production print shop.

The Document Company

To begin to mitigate this proprietary propensity, I established a task force with Chip Holt, Sandy Campbell, Ron Rider, Barb Pellow, John Lopiano, and

---

7   Interpress is a page description language (PDL) that was developed at Xerox PARC. It was designed for machine-to-machine communication; Xerox document preparation systems such as the Xerox Star and later, its PC-based desktop publishing package Ventura, generated Interpress masters to drive Xerox printers. Interpress was focused on the ability to process files quickly so that Xerox could feed its 120-page-per-minute print engines and keep them running at rated speed. This required knowledge of the capabilities of the target printer. John Warnock and Chuck Geschke believed there was a bigger market opportunity in a page-oriented PDL that could process complex pages without reference to the capabilities of a specific printer. As a result of this disagreement, the pair left Xerox and founded Adobe, with the PostScript PDL, which in the end won the day in terms of becoming an industry standard.

8   Xerox Network Systems (XNS) protocols were designed at Xerox PARC to be used across a wide variety of networked computing devices and office applications. It had some similarities to TCP/IP (Transmission Control Protocol/Internet Protocol) developed by the Defense Advanced Research Projects Agency (DARPA). A number of early networking companies, including 3Com, Ungermann-Bass and Novell, used XNS implementations. Each of these companies modified their implementation in some way, and its value as a standard was diminished. Like Interpress, XNS fell prey to an open market that adopted TCP/IP as a default network standard.

other selected executives to set a new systems direction for Xerox. We studied competitive, customer and industry trends. We identified opportunities to place both Xerox and partner digital front ends on new copier, printer, and systems products, including color devices. We looked at what happens to documents after they are "copied" and established a document finishing architecture that would allow us to connect inline to a wide range of finishing equipment from third party sources—booklet makers, binders and more. And we developed partnerships with others to drive applications and the associated print volume to the new DocuTech program.

We also created a document engagement strategy that reached out to include competitors, software partners, and customers. In short, we created a document systems architecture for Xerox that the company still depends on today. The DocuTech and its color successor, the iGen3, are still flagship products for Xerox nearly two decades after the DocuTech was introduced to the market.

A key part of this strategy was the adoption of industry standard communications protocols for all new high end products, including the DocuTech. This began taking Xerox down the path of becoming a credible systems company, rather than "just a copier company" and positioned the DocuTech as more than just a giant, supercharged copier. It also allowed us to take better commercial advantage of the wealth of knowledge and expertise that existed at PARC and other Xerox research sites in a way the company had never been able to do before. During this process, we reached out to many potential development partners for the DocuTech family, most of whom ultimately decided to join us.

This new systems architecture was my second major deployment of the Pragmatic Innovation strategy, with the IBM PC being the first. It had a major impact on Xerox's market positioning and future success with systems products.

Although we were not ready to go to market with a fully-enabled, open systems solution when the DocuTech was launched at New York's Javitts Center in October of 1990, we were ready to articulate our strategy for the product. We did so at the event with the help of a number of partners.[9] We demonstrated solutions with these software companies at our announcement using industry standards and our digital interface. In a way this was reminiscent of the early PC demo in the IBM Board Room.

Also at that event, a new identity for Xerox was announced; henceforth, the company would be known as Xerox, The Document Company, in an effort to put its "copier" identity behind it as it took advantage of the bigger opportunities offered by becoming a true player in the systems world. The Document Company moniker and a new, more modern logo were conceived by Len Vickers, who had been brought on board as Senior Vice President of Marketing. Vickers was known for coming up with GE's tagline, "We Bring Good Things to Life." Vickers did a great job of transitioning the company's image from The Copier Company to The Document Company and positioning it to assume a leadership role in the "systems" world.

The Print-On-Demand Market

The DocuTech with its concurrent operation and its scan-once-print-many capability launched a new era for the printing industry. Prior to the DocuTech, black & white copiers were used to produce relatively short runs of documents that didn't need extremely high quality, although the quality

---

9   Interestingly, one of those partners was Denise Miano, Founder and CEO of a small company that had been doing business with Xerox for some time. Her company, then known as New England Programming Services today exists as NEPS, where I am currently CEO and Denise is Chief Technology Officer. We are actively using the principles of Pragmatic Innovation to take NEPS into a new chapter of profitability and growth.

from copiers was generally quite good. If you needed thousands of copies and you wanted exceptional quality—perhaps because the document contained photos or graphics with fine lines—you would use an offset duplicator or offset press. Because of the need to make plates for the press, and the cost dynamics associated with press set-up, it was less expensive per copy the more copies you produced. That is, if you needed 50 copies of something, it would generally not make sense to produce those on an offset press. You were better served by estimating how many copies of a document you were likely to use over an extended period, produce all of those copies and store them in inventory to be distributed and used as needed.

For many applications, this was a good business practice. For example, receipt books, employment application forms, books, and manuals could be effectively managed this way. But as soon as a change was required in the content of those materials, costs could really mount up. Errata sheets could be manually added to a book or manual, or pages could be manually replaced. But more likely, obsolete materials were either used with outdated information, or they were simply thrown away.

Companies like Moore Corporation made a lot of money from this model. They would, at the behest of the customer, print thousands of forms, ostensibly to keep the cost per form as low as possible. The customer had the luxury of paying for those forms as they were used. But when it came time to obsolete those forms, the customer was presented with a bill for the rest of the printing as well as for the destruction of the obsolete materials—and that bill was often substantial.

The promise of the DocuTech was the ability to print just what you needed, when you needed it, and eliminate the entire problem of inventory obsolescence. Even if you performed significant manipulation of a document during its preparation, you could simply save the digital master for later reprinting. If a page needed to be substituted, no problem! Bring the stored file up on the DocuTech's touch screen, delete the offending page, scan in the new page and insert it. That created a brand-new document with all of the current information, and no obsolete inventory to dispose of.

This new capability was very well received in the high-tech industry. All of those black & white hardware and software manuals they were producing were easily transferable to a digital production process. Now they could add document production to their just-in-time manufacturing model. Just place a DocuTech at the end of the manufacturing line, and as the product came off the belt, you could produce its manual on the spot, pop it into the box, and you were ready to ship. This was a huge boon to a highly competitive industry where it was not uncommon to have to delay a product launch or shipment while waiting for the documentation to be printed. In order to prevent those delays, companies produced many more manuals than they needed in order to ensure they had enough on hand, which, of course, resulted in many of those manuals ending up in the landfill.

A Who's Who of Silicon Valley companies began to take advantage of print-on-demand, and within a few short years of the launch of the DocuTech, the market for black & white offset printing nearly dried up in Silicon Valley.

Of course, nothing ever stays static, and it wasn't too many years later that high-tech companies eliminated printed manuals altogether, opting for electronic distribution on CDs, and now often making manuals available only online. But there were plenty of other documents for those DocuTechs to produce. In fact, a well utilized DocuTech could easily crank out two to three million copies of high quality black & white printing each month, and many did.

The Xerox DocuTech Production Publisher, and its follow-on, the DocuTech Network Publisher, revolutionized the world of printing. Its effects are still being felt nearly 20 years later. This was a clear case of employing the principles of Pragmatic Innovation before the product came to market. We did our homework. We talked to customers and partners. We kept our eye on the competition. And we laid out a long-term strategy that would take us to the next level—color print on demand.

Setting the Stage for Color

Even though black & white printing is not a high growth market, the Xerox DocuTech is still a major contributor to Xerox revenues today, and it was the predecessor of the company's highly successful iGen3 digital production color press[10]. The systems architecture we laid out during the early days of the DocuTech allowed us to effectively begin the development of this next generation product, what our customers liked to call the color DocuTech and for which they were already clamoring when the DocuTech first hit the market.

The Xerox iGen3 was an instant success and won a prestigious GATF[11] InterTech Award in 2004. At the time, industry visionary and early purchaser of several iGen3's, Mike Panaggio of Daytona Beach, Florida's, DME, echoed the sentiment of many in the market when he said, "I fully believe that, decades from now, industry historians will recognize the introduction of the iGen3 press as the tipping point that swayed momentum to digital printing."[12]

Unlike the DocuTech, which gave birth to the digital on-demand printing market in black & white, the iGen3 leaped into a market that was already

---

10 In a speech delivered by Xerox Chairman & CEO Anne Mulcahy at drupa, a global printing show held in Düsseldorf, Germany, in May and June of 2008, she reported the installation of more than 2,000 iGen3's worldwide, the launch of its successor, the iGen4, and stated that according to research firm InfoTrends, about half of the world's digital color production pages were printed on Xerox devices.

11 Graphic Arts Technical Foundation (www.gain.net)

12 As reported in the July 30, 2004, issue of Output Links (www.OutputLinks.com)

populated with competitors but that had not reached its projected growth levels due to a number of things, but mostly due to price/performance and early problems with reliability. Even though the competition had been in the market ahead of Xerox for almost a decade, it didn't take long for this breakthrough product to gain a dominant market share with its benchmark price/performance and the significant weight of Xerox sales and marketing behind it. Xerox had also invested heavily in building a portfolio of partners to augment the iGen3 based on what the company learned during the early days of the DocuTech about the need to offer a wide range of internally and externally developed options in an open architecture environment.

These successes were directly related to the work we did in bringing the principles of Pragmatic Innovation to the Xerox Corporation. For a company that had such a rich history of innovation, it had not been able to successfully profit from that innovation for many years. But it was fertile ground for planting the seeds of Pragmatic Innovation. Much of the company's success today can be attributed to our ability to break out of old routines and bring breakthrough products like the systems-enabled DocuTech and iGen3 to market.

Microsoft and Xerox

Not all of my initiatives at Xerox were successful. Because of my previous work with Bill Gates and his team at Microsoft, I immediately saw the potential to leverage what I believed would be a market-dominating operating system—Microsoft Windows—to drive volume to Xerox devices. I engineered an agreement with Gates to incorporate scan, create, file, retrieve, store, and print commands in Windows. While this would not exclusively interface with Xerox devices, in the open standards world we were entering, we could partner with Microsoft in the early days of Windows to ensure that it natively implemented these commands, which I knew would be important to Xerox going forward as we brought more systems products to market and lived up to our new Document Company tag.

But this was a battle I lost. Xerox was still smarting from what it considered to be patent infringement on the part of Microsoft and Apple with respect to the GUI[13], mouse and other Xerox developments, and we would, in fact, file lawsuits that were ultimately unsuccessful because our suit had been filed too late. In addition, Xerox believed that once documents were scanned, it would be too difficult to retrieve them, even with the networked DocuTech of the future. In this environment, Xerox executives voted down any attempts to formalize such an arrangement. They also did not take advantage of their leadership scanning technology, although I tried to encourage an aggressive product development program in this area of the business.

The negotiations on the Microsoft side had not been easy, either. Early in Microsoft's history, Gates attempted to purchase a Xerox copier and was denied credit. It took many years for him to forgive that unfortunate decision.

Razors and Razor Blades

In pursuit of other applications for Pragmatic Innovation, my team and I analyzed revenue and profit models for both Xerox and its competitors. It was clear to me that Xerox could substantially improve both its profit picture and market share by taking a page out of HP's book. HP was quick to understand that it would make most of its money on supplies, not print engines. So the company priced print engines, particularly inkjet printers, low and made up for any profit shortfalls with HP inks and toners that carried substantial margins. My analysis of the Xerox model reflected that 4,000 percent of Xerox profits at the time came from the sale of supplies. I thought we could put a lid on HP at the departmental level, but my colleagues wanted

13 Graphical User Interface

to price based on tried and true copier techniques. Xerox was the premium price supplier of engines, generally priced 10 percent to 15 percent above market. I recommended aggressively pricing products operating at 40 pages per minute and above in order to place larger numbers of these units and sell more supplies. I felt this would position us well against HP, who was very successful with the smaller, low performance products but had not yet gained any significant market presence with faster printers. Unfortunately, I could not obtain agreement from the rest of the executive team on this approach, either.

When Is Enough Enough?

Xerox had not been able to grow its revenue stream very effectively. I thought that our development budget was large enough to enable us to introduce enough new products to increase our annual revenue generation by a factor of three. I felt that would ensure growth, but much to my surprise the organization did not want that much new product content. Sales in particular said that would be too expensive for them to deal with. I have never, before or since, had sales tell me they didn't want new products to sell. Rather, my experience was that sales always complained they didn't have enough product to sell!

Some is Better than None

Looking back at the Xerox years, I would say that some Pragmatic Innovation influence is better than none at all. When I assumed control of Worldwide Development and Manufacturing, I worked hard to implement Pragmatic Innovation within my domain and was able to achieve the successes outlined in this chapter. The process worked extremely well because it allowed Xerox to bring in new information from outside the company and to foster innovation from within. The result was the creation of a more efficient operating environment and an innovative systems strategy that relied on industry partners and new system implementation techniques. These processes allowed Xerox to take full advantage of Holt's DocuTech innovation, and in many ways, still permeates parts of the organization. Today, Xerox has well-developed partner programs with both customers and suppliers, but the company often appears to be more intent on controlling these relationships than on learning from them.

The bigger issue the company faces is that it still is led by people who built successful careers selling copiers. In fact, of Xerox' 29 corporate officers listed on their web site as we were writing this book, only four are new to the company in this century—three in Finance and the Chief Information Officer. The vast majority of the others started at Xerox in the 1970's or very early 1980's selling copiers; a few started in engineering positions in that timeframe. The company has not put in place a process to continue with a Pragmatic Innovation mindset, nor has it aggressively continued to seek new blood from outside the company. Xerox therefore is fairly inwardly focused and continues to miss significant opportunities which should be available to it. For a time, Xerox was aided by its decision to bring in experienced systems people from the outside, such as myself, Len Vickers, John Lopiano, and Al Dugan, and to leverage the wonderful energy of long-time employees like Chip Holt. But ultimately Xerox, like many big companies, reverted to form. The company neither consciously pursued Pragmatic Innovation in a way that continuously refreshed the organization, nor consciously injected people with outside experience into responsible positions within the company. Both are essential to keep an organization vital and competitive into the future.

While Anne Mulcahy has made a huge difference in the company since taking over the reins in 2000, there is still progress that could be made. Mulcahy, having come out of the Xerox sales environment, brings a "David

Kearns" feel back to the organization that had been missing under previous leadership. It remains to be seen what her legacy will be, but the outlook is more hopeful than it has been in some time.

Xerox has a broad portfolio of partners, but the company is known as difficult to work with, and potential partners sometimes walk away from the relationship in frustration. While the brain drain at Xerox is not as public as the defection of PARC researchers in the 1970s and 1980s, which gave birth to high profile Silicon Valley companies such as Adobe and 3Com, the brain drain continues nonetheless. Many companies have benefited from the bright, energetic, innovative individuals who have left Xerox to pursue opportunities in a more open environment, and many of those who choose to stay continue to promulgate the "business as usual" mental model of the Copier Company.

Nonetheless, the Xerox story is a significant success story for the Pragmatic Innovation process. While I had intuitively understood what needed to be done at IBM to carve out the microcomputer business and make it successful within the construct of a large, lumbering company, it was at Xerox that I began to put a formal process together that was repeatable, regardless of company or industry. A key element of that process is a SWOT analysis—Strengths, Weaknesses, Opportunities and Threats—that identifies internal opportunities, collects external information, and thoroughly analyzes the situation with an outcome of actionable steps that can be taken to move the organization forward. It is a critical element in establishing a culture of innovation within any company, and it begins to shift the focus from the inward, navel-gazing approach too many companies take, to a holistic approach that uses a much broader perspective. Since that time, I have successfully used this process more than 30 times with other enterprises. Chapter Eight of this book will give you a step-by-step process you can deploy in your own organization to achieve the kinds of positive results I have seen in almost every engagement.

At Xerox, we put together a strategy based on looking both inside and outside the company. We reached out to competitors, customers, and industry experts to build a plan. We deployed what I have learned to call the Pragmatic Innovation process. We began the process with a thoughtful review of Xerox's Strengths, Weaknesses, Opportunities and Threats (SWOT analysis). Then we identified the information we felt we needed to gather in order to really understand and pursue our opportunities.

This activity led us to understand what we needed to do to develop a connectivity strategy for our new products as well as what we need to do to develop and pursue color in both copying and printing

I remember one day when Barb Pellow remarked that when other companies wanted to be part of the success of the DocuTech, it was like magic. When you develop a good plan, based on a great product, others naturally want to be involved, and the whole becomes greater than the sum of the parts.

According to Chesbrough[14], Xerox is an active seller of its patents. Chesbrough examined patent reassignment applications from the top 19 firms in the IT sector based on the number of patents they reassigned during the period 1980 to 2003. Of Xerox reassignments, fully 53 percent were reassigned *outside the company*—likely sold or include with spin-offs—with only 4 percent of its reassigned patents coming from somewhere else. While this type of activity may generate revenue, it may not be the best approach for the long term. Xerox had a one billion dollar annual investment in development and technology in the early 1990s. You would have expected the company to exploit its technology investment for much higher returns. As a contrast, Nortel has taken the opposite approach, with 49 percent of

14 Chesbrough, Open Business Model, 2006

reassigned patents coming from outside the company (an active *buyer* of patents) and only 4 percent assigned out of the company. A deeper analysis of the Xerox practice would be interesting to undertake. But on the surface, it does appear that today's Xerox could benefit from a blended Open/Pragmatic Innovation approach that carefully considers the disposition of its IP in the context of a broader innovation schema.

We saw a no-nonsense approach to Pragmatic Innovation deployed by a very successful large company (IBM) that was stuck using a methodology best suited for its older products. IBM used internal mavericks and supported their efforts to drive new business based on a data-centric approach that took both an internal and an external view. With Xerox, senior management brought in fresh ideas in the form of new executive leadership as the catalyst to set a new direction. In both cases, the person at the top supported the growth initiatives and found leadership who could drive change. The process used in both cases was very similar. Over time this process has developed into an approach which has now successfully been deployed many, many times.

In the industry, there are many stories about IBMers who leave the company and find it difficult to operate outside of Big Blue. I felt I had been very fortunate to go to Xerox at a critical time in that company's development; I had a very positive and successful experience. When I heard there was an opportunity to become the CEO of a Fortune 500 company in a completely different industry (Gulfstream Aerospace) that was struggling with many of the same types of business issues I had helped address at IBM and Xerox, I responded to the challenge and moved on once again.

CHAPTER 4

Flying High at Gulfstream

"I want to stay as close to the edge as I can without going over.
Out on the edge you see all kinds of things you can't see from the center."

KURT VONNEGUT, JR. (1922-2007)

AMERICAN NOVELIST

I had both personal and business reasons for wanting to leave Xerox as 1991 dawned. We had experienced terrific market success with the DocuTech Production Publisher and the launch of the print on demand era. But with the departure of David Kearns from the picture, the energy, vitality and visionary leadership he provided departed as well. I had serious concerns about Paul Allaire's ability to make the right decisions for the future of the DocuTech. His management style, pure financial orientation and lack of vision were making it difficult to keep the momentum going.

Although it took several years for disaster to strike under Allaire's leadership, history reveals that it did indeed strike, and Xerox once again had to reinvent itself to maintain its place in the Fortune 500.

Meanwhile, I decided to contact Jerry Roche, CEO of Heidrich and Struggles, who had placed me at Xerox. I felt we had accomplished a great deal during my tenure with Xerox using the principles of Pragmatic Innovation. This philosophy was beginning to develop into a clearly defined and replicable process. I was looking for an opportunity in a more entrepreneurial environment where I could continue to develop these ideas and practices, ideally as CEO of a Fortune 500 company. Jerry set up a meeting for me with Gulfstream's owner, Teddy Forstmann of Forstmann Little, at its New York City offices in the GM building on 5th Avenue. The timing was right for Gulfstream, and I embarked on an adventure I could only have imagined in my wildest dreams.

But first, a little background on Gulfstream, including its history and a peek into its management style. As you will see, Gulfstream was a very internally-focused company that had done well for itself but needed a shot of innovation in order to move to the next level. I believed I was up to the challenge, but going into it, I had no idea how much of a challenge it would be. This was my opportunity to apply the principles of Pragmatic Innovation in an entirely new culture and industry. We accomplished some amazing things and had many unique and exciting experiences on the way, mixing with the world's rich and famous. It was also the first time I had worked with a venture firm like Forstmann Little, and the experience proved that Pragmatic Innovation could be applied with successful results in very different situations.

This chapter offers a history of Gulfstream, including the leveraged buyout environment under which the company was operating when I joined. It delineates the Pragmatic Innovation process we undertook and the results we achieved. The stories that are integrated into the chapter will provide a unique view of the company by documenting many of the fascinating people and places Cristina and I were able to experience during my tenure there. It was an adventure, and I hope you will enjoy the vicarious ride.

The Gulfstream Story

Gulfstream was founded in 1958 by Grumman Aviation and located at the airport in Savannah, Georgia. The first plane marketed under the Gulfstream brand was a twin turbo-prop aircraft called the Gulfstream I. It was the first jet designed exclusively as a business aircraft. In addition, a large number of the standard fuselage Gulfstream I's were used as commuter airliners, seating up to 24 passengers. Military Gulfstream I's were built for the US Navy (navigator training TC-4s) and US Coast Guard (VIP VC-4s). The Coast Guard also used Gulfstream jets for executive transport. Two hundred Gulfstream I's were built and sold.

The Gulfstream II, launched in 1966, was a two-engine business jet and the first large-cabin business jet. It had a ceiling of 45, 000 feet and could carry between 12 and 19 passengers. The GII was not capable of transatlantic or cross country missions in the United States. In addition to its business applications, it was used by the Moroccans, Oman, and the Venezuelan military, as well as the U.S. Coast Guard and U.S. Army.

The Gulfstream III was introduced in 1983. This aircraft began to make long-range missions possible. In addition to private business use, many countries used the plane for selected military missions.

The Gulfstream IV was announced in 1988 and supported in earnest what became known as the Jet Set. It had a range of 3,767 nautical miles. From

Hollywood to Wall Street to the oil fields of Saudi Arabia, ownership of a Gulfstream GIV jet was a status symbol for the world's rich and famous—as well as leading corporations. It allowed missions across the Atlantic and transcontinentally across North America in both directions. Eastbound trans-Pacific missions were possible under good conditions. This airplane was the foundation for the "Jet Set."

This series of four product introductions over a period of nearly 20 years built Gulfstream's reputation as the maker of the biggest, fastest, and most expensive corporate jets in the world.

Allen E. Paulson

No story about Gulfstream would be complete without understanding a bit about Allen E. (Al) Paulson. I have read many different accounts relating how Al Paulson ended up at Gulfstream. My version is based on personal conversations he and I had, so I can only assume it is accurate.

In 1978, Grumman decided to get out of the business jet field. Grumman had put Gulfstream on the market because the U.S. government was uncomfortable with the company's overseas sales practices for these private jets. Grumman did not want to put its lucrative U.S. jet fighter business in jeopardy. Al was able to acquire Gulfstream for $52 million using significant leverage from funds borrowed from Kirk Kerkorian, a friend of his. Al, an aerospace entrepreneur, combined the former Grumman operation with two other small-plane manufacturers to form a new company which he named Gulfstream Aerospace.

Between 1978 when he acquired the company, and 1991 when his day-to-day operational relationship with the company was severed, it is impossible to separate the story of Gulfstream from the story of Al Paulson. Al was born in Iowa in 1922. He left school at the age of 12 and joined the Air Force before he was 18 years of age. He developed his knowledge about and love for airplanes through his service career as an aircraft mechanic. After many post-military work experiences, he founded his first company in 1951, selling surplus aircraft parts.

By 1978, Al had attained a level of success in his business activity. He had also acquired a push-pull aircraft design that he wanted to pursue. So he started looking to acquire a company that could advance his business success and provide a platform for launching the new aircraft design. At that time, Grumman had put Gulfstream on the market because of its U.S. government concerns, cited above, and Al was able to acquire the company. Over the years, he made a great deal of money through his many Gulfstream financial dealings.

Al proceeded to make a career out of buying and refinancing Gulfstream over and over, to his tremendous personal financial advantage. The timeline was something like this.

Gulfstream Timeline

- 1978: Leveraged the original acquisition of Gulfstream from Grumman ($52 million).

- 1983: IPO of Gulfstream based on the GIII announcement

- 1985: Took the company private, selling Gulfstream to Chrysler for $637 million

- 1990: Played a role in the sale of Gulfstream from Chrysler to Forstmann/Little ($850 million); retained a 32 percent stake

- 1992: Al withdraws from active management, sells stock to Forstmann Little for $50 million. Retained seat on the Board.

1992: Gulfstream announces GIV S/P and GV

1996: Gulfstream undertakes IPO, raising $1 billion. 1996 record earnings of $47 million, up 63 percent over preceding year, driven by demand for G V and participation in partial ownership programs

1996: Gulfstream sold to General Dynamics

In 1985, Al sold Gulfstream to Chrysler Corporation for $637 million. At 68 years of age, he stayed on to run the business for Chrysler. In 1990, the company again changed hands when Paulson joined forces with Theodore J. (Teddy) Forstmann and his company, Forstmann Little, to purchase Gulfstream for $850 million. As a result of that deal, Paulson continued as chairman and CEO with a 32 percent stake; Forstmann Little retained the balance of ownership (68 percent).

Teddy Forstmann is best known as a Wall Street dealmaker who, as the dominant partner of Forstmann Little & Co., helped invent the leveraged buyout in the 1980's.

Al built his financial position through Gulfstream, along with a number of auto dealerships he owned in California. He also became very successful in horse racing, with his career as an owner and breeder beginning in 1980. He became the largest thoroughbred horse breeder in the world with farms in Kentucky, Florida, California, and France. His best-known horse was Cigar, who in 1995-96, tied the modern record for consecutive wins and set a record for lifetime earnings at nearly $10 million.[1]

Al died in 2000.

---

1 Allen Paulson obituary, About.com, July 20, 2000

Joining Gulfstream

In May of 1991, I was named President and Chief Operating Officer of Gulfstream, and I also played an advisory role with Forstmann Little, including a seat on the Board of General Instruments. I quickly learned more than I ever wanted to know about the Forstmann Little leveraged model. The company's approach was to purchase low-cap companies leveraged with bank debt, operate them successfully while paying interest-only on the bank debt, and then take them public, promising investors that interest payments would be converted to profits after an IPO. During the time I worked for Forstmann Little, some of the companies under management included Pullman, The Topps Company (sports cards), General Instruments, and Callaway Golf Clubs.

Forstmann Little planned to follow this leveraged model with the Gulfstream acquisition, a deal that was facilitated by Al Paulson. But it didn't quite work out as planned. A 1997 *Business Week* cover story[2] describes the situation:

> To Ted Forstmann, Gulfstream began as just another deal—a "conventional 1980s-style leveraged buyout," as he puts it now. "The idea was that we'd cut costs here and there, sell 10 more planes a year, and make a good return on investment," Forstmann says. "We thought it would be a piece of cake."

> But Forstmann and his partners would eat crow, not cake, for they failed to recognize the deepening problems that were even then gnawing away at Gulfstream. Far from being a good candidate for a quick tune-up and a lucrative sale back to the public, Gulfstream was a capital-intensive, old-line enterprise in need of a sweeping and costly overhaul.

---

2   Gulfstream's Pilot, *Business Week Magazine*, April 17, 1997 (Cover Story)

The success of the GIV jet was what initially stimulated Forstmann Little's interest in the company and was the underlying driver for its acquisition from Chrysler. The $850 million deal was comprised of $750 million in debt that was supported by only $100 million in equity[3]. Though additional investments were made in the company over the ensuing few years, little was ever applied to debt reduction.

But shortly after acquiring the company, Teddy realized that he needed a different level of professional management than Al Paulson could provide. He was searching for a new CEO who could help him undertake the comprehensive reform that he quickly learned the company required. That is where I came into the picture through my relationship with Jerry Roche.

Thus, when I came on board, I found a company that had a wide range of very significant financial and organizational problems.

Bill and Cristina with Brian and Judy Little at the Paris Airshow

—shortly after joining Gulfstream

---

3   *Gulfstream's Pilot*, by Anthony Bianco with William C. Symonds. *Business Week*, April 14, 1997

Market Leader Poised for a Fall

Although I was new to the aerospace industry, I was not new to the world of private jets. During my previous seven years of business assignments, I had a corporate jet available for my use. While I was running the Personal Computer business at IBM, I had access to a chartered Lear jet, and I had a Canadair Challenger at my disposal while I worked at Xerox. Although I was not a pilot, I appreciated how much more effective you could be when you could travel without the restrictions of commercial airline schedules and the delays and travails associated with commercial air travel. Meeting with and entertaining customers on board a private jet also offered some unique advantages for an executive. I also found the Xerox Canadair a convenient way to save time by sleeping on board overnight between meetings. I had also previously traveled on IBM's Gulfstream and appreciated what a fine product the GIV was.

Prior to accepting the position with Gulfstream, I had not visited its Savannah headquarters. All of our meetings were held in other locations. Teddy made Forstmann Little's Gulfstream jet available to me for my first trip to Savannah. Little did I know I was in for a bit of a shock. While the Gulfstream jet is the ultimate in luxury, the Gulfstream headquarters were old and tired. Offices were crowded into a cement block building with few frills, and the company was using a number of temporary trailers whose life had obviously been extended beyond their initial temporary role. The manufacturing facility was functional and had high quality standards every step of the way, but the manufacturing process was extremely low tech. It took the better part of a year to build a GIV.

Gulfstream jets are sold "green." This means they have no interior finishing and minimal electronics. At the time, list price for a GIV was $25 million, and the combination of custom finishing of the interior and electronics package cost in the range of $3 million to $10 million, dependent upon the tastes and requirements of the customer. Gulfstream had a talented cadre of craftsmen who performed the finishing and paint work that turned the green aircraft into a work of art.

In addition to manufacturing, Gulfstream performed maintenance of its fleet in Savannah, as well as at a facility in Long Beach, California.

Another surprise I encountered at the Savannah facility was the age and tenure of the staff. The team had clearly been with Gulfstream for a long time; and the executive team was all male, white and over 65, a dramatic change from what I had grown used to at IBM and Xerox. Many of these people were, of course, terrific and knowledgeable resources. This included Charlie Coppi, who headed up development starting with the Gulfstream I all the way through the Gulfstream IV.

Looking Inward

The basic Gulfstream jet was based on a 1960's design. As new models were introduced, they included new propulsion systems and advancements in electronics. There were longer models available that carried more fuel, and other refinements had been added, like winglets for longer range. But in comparison to the environment I had come from—even as stale and stodgy as IBM and Xerox could seem at times—Gulfstream was not a company that was investing in its future. Nor was it focused on what its competition was doing.

The company did little marketing, depending instead upon high profile sales agents like Mohamed El Fayad, whose sales territory was Saudi Arabia and Brunei; or Bernard Duc, Senior Partner HMI Ltd (Hong Kong) and Deputy Chairman of the Rolls-Royce South East Asia Advisory Board, who had relationships with Dr. Habibi in Djakarta, the then-leader of Indonesia; the leadership in the Philippines; and the Royal Family of Thailand. In these cases, each decision to buy a jet produces a large commission for the agent. The company also depended on participation in semi-annual air shows in Paris, France, and Farnborough UK, as well as the annual National Business Aircraft Association (NBAA) show, to peddle its wares.

Like many successful companies, the Gulfstream of that period was convinced it held the number one position in the industry and found no need to assess its competition on an ongoing basis. I could immediately see that significant investments would be required to ensure the future success of Gulfstream, but somehow Al Paulson had managed to convince Teddy that Forstmann Little's normal leveraged approach would work in this instance. I had my doubts from the beginning of my association with the company.

Under the Radar

In 1991, in addition to focusing on growing sales for Gulfstream and learning the business, I took the initiative to repeat what I had done at IBM and Xerox. I assembled a team to develop a strategic plan for Gulfstream based on information from both inside and outside the company. The team was led by Bob Coman, a bright young man who had been managing government contracts for the company. Also on the team were operational level people from throughout the company who had direct experience with customers. One of these was Helen Newman from the Washington D.C. office, who was one of the best sales and customer liaison professionals I have ever met.[4]

---

4 Helen Newman had been Executive Assistant to Carl Albert when he was Speaker of the House of Representatives. She literally knew everyone who mattered in Washington

With any Pragmatic Innovation initiative, people from outside the company are critical to ensuring an open mind about the business and its opportunities and threats. Gulfstream was no different, and I sought personnel from outside the company to bring that perspective. Those included Kevin Russell, who joined the company as a member of the sales team and contributed to the task force. Another was Thomas P. Maletta, who came to Gulfstream from Xerox and took on responsibility for Finance. We added Henry Ogrodzinski, responsible for external communications. We also took advantage of external consultants to give us a good perspective from outside the company.

As I had done in the past, we started the process with an interactive SWOT analysis, identifying both what we knew about the company's situation and the information we needed to acquire in order to take a fresh look at the company and the industry. Appendix A of this book provides a thorough questionnaire that embodies many of the types of questions the team needs to explore. As you launch your own Pragmatic Innovation initiatives, you can use this example to help you quickly put together your own questionnaire for task force members to complete prior to the initial task force meeting. This process will streamline information gathering and allow the team to quickly identify information or knowledge gaps.

To some extent, our work at Gulfstream went on in the background without a lot of engagement on the part of Teddy and the Board. I wanted to come to them with a complete story in order to head off the natural objections I knew I would face. As President of the company, I had the latitude to operate in this manner and was the executive sponsor for the initiative.

---

and played a critical role at Gulfstream, where 20 percent of our business came from U.S. government sales, with another 40 percent coming from foreign sales that required U.S. government approval due to security concerns.

The Findings

We did find a number of gaps in our operational mentality. By backing those findings with facts and data, it was a much easier sell to Teddy and the Board than it would have been had I simply based recommendations on my opinions, especially as a newcomer to the industry. Here is what we discovered.

1. Within Gulfstream, there was no awareness that Canadair was eroding our market share and was beginning to be perceived by many as the industry leader. The company had been improving the operating characteristics of its Challenger aircraft so that it had nearly the same range as the GIV but with a green price of about $14 million, significantly lower than the GIV's $25 million green price tag. In addition, the Challenger had a larger fuselage diameter, making it a more comfortable airplane.

   Canadair had been acquired by Bombardier, Inc. of Montreal, Canada in 1986. Bombardier had also acquired de Havilland, Learjet, and Short Brothers, three other manufacturers of small planes. This consolidation and backing further boosted Canadair's competitive threat to Gulfstream. While there were other competitors emerging, such as Dassault Aviation of France, the maker of the Falcon corporate jet, Canadair was the primary threat.

   Paulson's response to competitive activity was to slash prices and offer special deals that cut significantly into Gulfstream's margins. It treated the symptoms, not the disease.

2. Canadair had begun touting a future product—Global Express—an aircraft that could fly non-stop from New York to Hong Kong and from Riyadh to Washington D.C. These were generally considered to be two of the most important routes for future private plane development. The combination of the Challenger's price/performance and the potential offered by the new Global Express were influencing commercial customers' intentions, often pushing them toward purchase of a Canadair instead of a Gulfstream. The team recommended development of a competitive product, which we called the GV. This product would take a half billion dollar investment and four years. But the team felt it was necessary in order to regain the number one position in the industry.

3. Al Paulson and Forstmann Little, on the other hand, had been touting their own future product, based on a joint project being explored between Gulfstream and the Sukhoi Design Bureau in Moscow. Their plan was to build a supersonic business jet. After reviewing this initiative, the team came to the conclusion that this project was probably not commercially viable for a number of reasons I will discuss in a bit. They felt that further investigation was required to determine whether, in fact, the project was practical and then Gulfstream needed to proceed accordingly.

4. The team identified several enhancements that could be made to the GIV to give it new sales life and better position it against the competition. This included a boost in range with a new model called the GIV S/P (Special Product—a nomenclature I

borrowed from the PC) and a new internal finishing approach to provide more usable room inside the barrel of the GIV that we called a "Wide-Inside" finishing approach.

5. The team recommended investigating involvement in a new approach to partial private plane ownership that was being promoted by NetJets[5] of Woodbridge, New Jersey, founded by Richard Santulli in 1986. We believed this project, which was uncovered by Kevin Russell, could be a stimulus to sales.

Along the way, we also determined that we needed to establish better marketing techniques that investigated customer requirements and played to those requirements for better receptivity among our prospects.

It was the recommendation of the team that taking action on these findings would help Gulfstream performance both in the short and long term. They would, however, require more capital investment, which was not compatible with the Forstmann Little business model. But it was our considered opinion that the SP and Wide-Inside models would stimulate immediate sales and that the GV would preserve Gulfstream's leadership franchise.

However, prior to making a recommendation to Teddy and the Board, we needed to complete our work regarding the supersonic business jet project.

A Visit to E-Systems

A remarkable learning experience for me during the course of this task force was a visit to E-Systems, a company in Plano, Texas.

---

5 As of this writing NetJets is still operating, as a Berkshire Hathaway company (www. NetJets.com). NetJets created the concept of fractional plane ownership, giving businesses and individuals all of the benefits of jet ownership at a fraction of the cost.

Among other things, E-Systems performs specialized development work on privately owned planes. The purpose of the visit was to learn what customers were doing with our planes—and others—after they purchased them.

During my visit to E-Systems, I had the opportunity to view Saudi King Fahd's 747, which was finished very differently than any other 747 I had ever seen! The King's private quarters were located upstairs behind the cockpit. In the forward section on the lower level of this particular plane was a hookah, or water pipe, surrounded by cushions. Beyond that was a very large conference room with a table that could easily seat 15 to 20 people. The next section had business class type seating for staff. Behind that was the operating room and the "Live Donor Quarters." Apparently, the King generally travels with a medical team and a perfectly matched donor in case spare parts are needed. This was not something we could accommodate on a Gulfstream!

Breaking Barriers

As mentioned earlier, there had been much discussion by Al Paulson, and later Forstmann Little, about developing a supersonic business jet in partnership with the Sukhoi Design Bureau in Moscow. In fact, Al and the Sukhoi Bureau Chief had held a press conference at the Paris Air Show to discuss the venture. This was during Perestroika, and Sam Nunn, the Senator from Georgia, was a key player in Foreign Relations and Defense. He supported programs that would help the Soviets take advantage of their military investments to promote commercial enterprise and was very interested in this potential project.

Touring the Gulfstream Plant with Senator Sam Nunn

I took a team to Moscow to review the project's potential. The trip was an eye-opener, to say the least. At the time, the first McDonald's restaurant had just opened in Moscow, and lines to purchase food there wound around the block. Fast food was a totally new concept for the Russians.

We stayed at a nice hotel, and I took the Sukhoi people to dinner. We were presented with a very nice menu. As each individual chose items, we were told they were not available. Eventually you discovered that they only had a chicken dish that day. We saw that process repeated constantly. It was an interesting transition to a free economy.

I discovered that the Sukhoi Bureau was accustomed to getting Administration support for pretty much anything it wanted to do. The Bureau was proposing a plane that used the MiG-29 propulsion system to drive a supersonic business jet and had recommended a plane with a 5.5-foot diameter. In their view, this would not present height problems for customers. They also did not think there would be any issues with sonic noise over land masses, and that the very short life of MiG-29 engines before failure—15 to 20 flying hours—should not be a problem either. In other words, they really had no grip on Western-based business considerations, critical to being able to sell a plane into those markets.

I also found that, like the Shanghai Xerox plant I had visited a few years earlier, the Russians had a very limited concept of preventative maintenance. That applied not only to the aircraft engines, but across the board. When I landed at the Sheremetyevo airport in Moscow, I saw literally hundreds of planes in the infield between the runways whose sole purpose was to serve as a source for scavenging parts for other aircraft. This behavior was not limited to the airport. You saw it everywhere—autos, even buildings. The Soviet Union had no culture of preventative maintenance, a common theme in a lot of Third World countries.

Finally, I was shocked at the lack of computing power this elite research and development organization had. When I was running the IBM PC business, I could never really understand the U.S. government's position on exporting computers, especially when we wanted to sell older surplus PCs behind the Iron Curtain. My visit to Moscow demonstrated what a devastating effect this restrictive export policy had on Soviet development. They did not have enough distributed computing power to do simulations, and as a result they had to build the world's largest wind tunnel to test planes. They actually placed weights on airplane wings until they broke off because that was the only way they could test them.

The team ultimately concluded that the supersonic business jet project was not practical. I reported this finding to Sam Nunn, and the project essentially just dropped out of the Gulfstream talk tracks.

Interestingly, more than a decade later, Allen Paulson's son, Michael, resurrected the supersonic business jet concept. An article in the January 2005 edition of *Airport Journals* reported:

Two companies believe the future for civil supersonic travel is sooner rather than later, but it remains to be seen which one will be successful. Billionaire investor Robert Bass backs Reno-based Aerion Corporation. The company is placing its bets on its natural laminar flow technology developed and patented by Dr. Richard Tracy. Simultaneously, Supersonic Aerospace International, led by Michael Paulson, is continuing the legacy of late Gulfstream founder Allen Paulson. SAI revealed at NBAA its secret three-year project to develop a Quiet Supersonic Transport, which relies on sonic boom mitigation for future success.

Both supersonic projects claim the capacity for eight to 12 passengers, a range of 4,000 nautical miles, sales prices of $80 million and entry into service by 2012. Both Aerion and SAI are pressing hard to demonstrate economic viability to investors and potential industrial partners, including airframe manufacturers.

The SAI project continues Al's legacy. He left funds in trust for Michael to use for the project. The article quotes Michael as saying, "He knew that subsonic transportation was going to reach a wall. We believe that we've already hit that wall. You cannot tweak the current line of business jets any further. You can change the avionics a little, but the only revolutionary way to change transportation is to go supersonic and make it available to the business and government transportation markets." SAI's management team at the time anticipated a market for 300 to 400 aircraft over the next 10 to 15 years, according to the article.

As of this writing, the company is still promoting its Quiet Supersonic Transport technology. The company has placed Lockheed Martin's famed "Skunk Works" under contract to help them further develop the technology.

The Gulfstream Board Weighs In

The Gulfstream Board had some very impressive members. It included Teddy Forstmann, of course, and Brian Little. It also included George Schultz, former Secretary of State; Don Rumsfeld, former Secretary of Defense (twice!), Drew Lewis, former Secretary of Transportation, Roger Penske, and other business leaders. These people were a great source of experience, advice, and business and government contacts.

The results of our team's strategy work were presented to the Board. Despite the time and investment required to implement our suggestions, which flew directly in the face of Forstmann Little's normal business practices and would require some refinancing, the Board approved proceeding with the GIV SP, the announcement of the GV, and the scrapping of the supersonic business jet project. With Board approval, we also put immediate plans in place to improve our sales and marketing activity to circumvent the need for the aggressive pricing levels our competition had driven us to.

By this time, I had been appointed Chairman, CEO and President of Gulfstream in an effort by Teddy to further distance Al Paulson from the business.

Taking Gulfstream Public—Almost

As 1991 progressed and it appeared that we were on target to exceed our sales plan for GIV's, Teddy decided to attempt a public offering in early 1992 using Morgan Stanley to manage the deal. In this way, he could have access to a source of additional funding that would allow us to make the investments required to bring Gulfstream up to snuff and to ensure its future competitive positioning. Also important to Teddy was the fact that this approach would enable him to acquire funding without the sad state of affairs at Gulfstream becoming public knowledge. In other words, it would allow him to save face and maintain his reputation as a smart financier and savvy businessman.

In 1991, we had a plan to sell 28 GIVs; we actually sold 31. I would later have reason to wish I had sandbagged a little, keeping a couple of them in my pocket for 1992.

The IPO was scheduled to close in early April of 1992, but soft first quarter sales indicated that the opening price was more likely to be $12 per share than the $20 Teddy was looking for. So Teddy pulled the offering at the last minute and was back to square one in terms of how he would finance the necessary investments while still retaining some level of satisfaction among Gulfstream's investors and the Board.

Interestingly, Teddy ended up proceeding with a General Instruments IPO three months later at a lower-than-targeted price. The company was run by Don Rumsfeld. Teddy was looking for $18 per share, and it looked like it would end up at $12. Teddy could not afford two failed IPOs, and General Instruments was the beneficiary of that situation. Rumsfeld told me he considered himself lucky that Gulfstream had gone first.

Part of the reason for soft sales in 1992 was an action by Presidential candidate, then President-Elect, Clinton. During the campaign, he placed significant focus on a need to eliminate private aircraft, which he felt were luxury items, not necessities. He proposed tax actions against companies who used private jets. When he won the election, it froze our sales. We ended 1992 with sales of something like 24 jets, which was a huge disappointment.

Enjoying the Glamour and Sizzle

I have so many Gulfstream stories about our experiences traveling and doing business with the world's rich and famous that it is not possible to share them all here. But I would like to touch on a few highlights I think you will find interesting.

Mohamed El Fayad

Mohamed El Fayad was incredibly kind to both Cristina and me, especially when he heard about our wedding plans. Mohamed was Gulfstream's executive sales representative serving King Fahd's regime and the Sultan of Brunei. These two were perfect customers for our business model. Mohamed did a fabulous job for the company, and I enjoyed my interactions with him. When I visited him at Harrods in London, he personally showed me how he had put his face on all the Sphinx's in the Egyptian Gallery, and how he harpooned Tiny Roland, his old nemesis, in a display in the Seafood shop.

He allowed us to use his personal helicopter when we traveled in England. When he learned that Cristina and I were honeymooning at the Hotel du Cap in southern France, he invited us to a memorable lunch on his yacht in St. Tropez. He sent a limousine for us, but with the horrendous traffic in the area, it took forever for us to arrive at the yacht. Mohamed was disconcerted by what he perceived as a great inconvenience for us.

His wife and four younger children joined us on board for lunch. It was a lengthy lunch, and when it was time for us to return, Mohamed contacted Dodi Fayad, his elder son, who was cruising in the harbor, to take us back to our origination point across the bay. Dodi had just acquired a small Navy destroyer which he had modified for his personal use, with state-of-the-art music systems and speakers. The top deck had been converted into a wonderful place to entertain friends. Later this boat would become more well-known as a result of Dodi's friendship with Princess Diana.

Dodi took us back up the coast of France with tremendous speed and style—a much faster and more pleasant trip than the limo ride. Our memories of Dodi are of a young man full of enthusiasm, laughter, friendliness, and kindness who went out of his way to make this small journey so special during our special honeymoon getaway.

When visiting Mohamed's office in London, he showed us the Oscars he and his son had been awarded for Chariots of Fire and Hook. When our daughter, Gabriela, was born, one of the first gifts we received was a special Harrod's teddy bear from Mohamed. He and his family still retain a special place in our hearts.

Bernard Duc

Bernard Duc was another sales agent who handled the Far East. He had been a leader in the French military and Parliament and had been present at the end of Dien Bien Phu. He had been knighted in Thailand by the Crown Prince. Bernard represented Gulfstream, Rolls Royce Engines and Riva boats and had personal offices in Paris, Spain, London, and Hong Kong.

We went on a long trip with Bernard through the Far East. We made sales calls on Dr. Habibi in Djakarta, the Crown Prince and Prime Minister of Thailand, military leadership in the Philippines, and individual prospects in Hong Kong and Tokyo. Most of our days were spent in meetings and our evenings entertaining key customers, sometimes with our spouses. For me, it was a particularly special trip, as I now was taking my new daughter, Gabriela, on her first extended trip at four months of age. The long Easter weekend occurred in the middle of our trip, so after our stay in Djakarta, we went to Bali for a much-needed three-day break with Bernard and several Gulfstream staff members. Gabriela's first swimming pool was attached to our room at the Four Seasons in Bali.

We stayed at the Hilton Suite in Djakarta and the Oriental Suite at the Oriental Hotel in Bangkok, and we were in good company. After signing the guest book for each suite, we noticed that some of the most recent guests included Margaret Thatcher, Ronald Reagan, and the Rolling Stones. This trip resulted in two sales.

Bernard Duc had created an incredible and effective marketing strategy and a magnificent lifestyle for himself. I found him to be diligent, effective and fun to be with, and he seemed to be able to keep most of his activities under the radar.

Announcing the GV

A key facet of our strategy was to recapture market leadership from Canadair. We had to overcome the price/performance characteristics of the Challenger and the possible future of the Global Express. In the private jet industry, hints and innuendoes regarding future actions were the rule as companies wanted absolute certainty of customer support before announcing new products and making the huge investments that were required to develop and launch them. That was not the world I had traveled in previously. We moved quickly to announce the GIV S/P, and we decided to announce the GV at the Farnborough Air Show and at that year's NBAA in Dallas.

Mohamed was a co-owner of the Dorchester Hotel in London with the Sultan of Brunei and graciously granted us use of the facility for the launch party. We invited all of our best customers in Europe and the Middle East to a formal announcement party, with Michael Crawford of "Phantom of the Opera" fame and his leading lady to entertain.

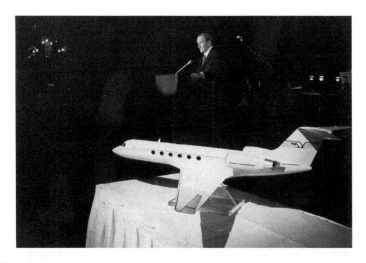

The following day, we announced the G-V at the Air Show along with our plan to use the new BMW/Rolls Royce engines for this jet. This would be the first time jet propulsion systems would be produced in Germany since the end of World War I.

CEO of BMW/Rolls Royce announcing the GIV at the Farnsborough Air Show

Several months later we held another announcement party in Dallas at the NBAA show. This time, our best customers were entertained by Bill Cosby. Bill and I were at Temple and Lafayette, respectively, at the same time, and we had faced off in basketball games. Bill was a Gulfstream owner, and we worked out a plan for him to entertain our guests in exchange for maintenance on his plane. This was a terrific opportunity for Cristina and I to meet a really nice, funny, and very special man.

Bill Cosby with Cristina and Gabriela before the Dallas announcement

During the Gulfstream period, Cristina and I spent a great deal of time traveling, including numerous trips to Europe, We entertained customers at The World Economic Forum in Davos, Switzerland, and at the Winter Olympics in Grenoble, France. We visited Kuwait City two days after the end of the first Gulf War to replace a GIV that the Iraq army had ruined.

Cristina in Kuwait City—one day after the first Gulf War ended

These adventures were memorable and fun. But they were accompanied by significant challenges as the situation at Gulfstream became more difficult.

Moving On

With the failed IPO, soft sales and the need to invest significant time and dollars to guarantee Gulfstream's market position, 1992 ended up being a lot less fun than the previous year. Teddy was under pressure, and all of us felt it.

Over the next several months, I had three key meetings with Teddy at The '21' Club in New York. During the first meeting, he told me he was going to sever his relationship with Brian Little.

At the second meeting, we discussed the difficulty he was facing in repackaging the financing message without losing the confidence of his limited partners.

At the third meeting, he informed me he would be announcing that Brian Little, Don Rumsfeld and I were leaving the organization at the same time he planned to proceed with the refinancing activity. Those announcements were made in November of 1993, and Teddy named himself Chairman of Gulfstream, running the company until he could bring in a replacement.

The Effects of Pragmatic Innovation at Gulfstream

Although my tenure at Gulfstream was relatively short, by embarking on the Pragmatic Innovation process right out of the chute, we managed to make significant progress in a very short time. By doing so, I learned that this process was portable to industries other than computing and communications. I was also able to play the role of the executive sponsor, a role that had been played by Frank Carey and David Kearns during my efforts at IBM and Xerox, respectively. Part of the continued success I attribute to these two individuals and what I learned from watching them act in this role.

We blended the best of Gulfstream with good people from the outside. We utilized operational executives to drive the process, rather than the senior executive team that had previously driven the company's decisions. We reached out to customers, business partners, and competitors to gather facts upon which to base our conclusions and recommendations. We used this fact-based approach to sell our new ideas to the Board and gained its support despite the fact that these changes required a definitive shift in business model for the company under Teddy's leadership.

The Gulfstream experience demonstrated that Pragmatic Innovation was an industry-agnostic, replicable process that delivers results and could be used in many different situations. The base work we accomplished allowed Teddy to do what he did best—packaging financing and spinning the story to the market. Among other things, the base work our team accomplished laid the groundwork for improvement in the GIV manufacturing process. The introduction of the two new models injected new life into the GIV family while the four-year development process of the GV was underway. It also put the kibosh on the supersonic business jet program, which would have been a disaster for the company, replacing that initiative with what turned out to be a very successful GV development project. In fact, by the time I left Gulfstream, we had 41 GV orders on the books with nonrefundable deposits.

Despite the fact that my relationship with the company was severed, Gulfstream continued down the path that our team had delineated for the company, with great success. Although the situation at the company was grim in mid-1993 and refinancing was required to build a new future, by 1996 the financial picture was excellent, and the GV was ready to launch. In fact, enough GV orders were already in hand to allow Teddy to finally take the company public, which he did in October 1996, raising $1 billion in one of the largest IPOs of that year. True to form, though, only about 10 percent of that money was rolled back into Gulfstream to continue to strengthen the company. However, Teddy's investors were happy, having ended up with a return on their investment in line with Teddy's historical objectives.

Later that year, the company was rescued from this fate. The successful IPO triggered interest in Gulfstream from General Dynamics, who acquired the company and still owns it today.

After my adventures at Gulfstream, I moved on to NEBS. I had served on the NEBS board since 1988, and they were looking for a new President & CEO. My appointment to that role was announced the same day I left Gulfstream.

As I look back on the NEBS experience, it was the most dynamic example of how Pragmatic Innovation can revolutionize a company, even in a contracting and competitive market such as business forms. While it doesn't sound nearly as exciting as inventing the IBM PC, launching the era of print on demand, or flying with the world's rich and famous, from a business perspective, it was one of the most rewarding experiences in my career as you will see in Chapter Five.

CHAPTER 5

Forming a New Future

As the previous chapters have highlighted, my efforts were involved with large corporate enterprises in multiple business arenas. My major efforts as a Fortune 500 executive had extended over two decades of exciting technological evolution in a variety of rapidly adapting industries. My next career efforts were directed toward smaller, even entrepreneurial, organizations with more limited resources and revenues invested in innovation or development, but equally promising in the nature of their business. With three successful Pragmatic Innovation experiences under my belt, I was excited about the prospect of taking my executive skill sets to the first of these smaller enterprises, a company I had known well, having sat on its Board of Directors for many years. The prospect of bringing Pragmatic innovation to New England Business Service (NEBS) as the CEO piqued my interest in 1993.

NEBS was a truly family-grown business. As many small businesses begin with vision of a founder that recognizes a business need, so was the case with NEBS. Al Anderson was a forms salesman based in Cleveland, Ohio. In 1952, he realized that there was a need for customized forms in small quantities to serve small businesses such as dry cleaners, beauty shops, small retailers, and others. These businesses were purchasing generic forms and customizing them, if at all, using a rubber stamp. Anderson believed he could build a business serving this need. He also realized that he could not effectively support such a business using direct sales, since the niche he was after was fragmented and widely distributed. So he turned to direct mail marketing as the most efficient sales mechanism for addressing this market. He focused his sales efforts on smaller businesses—those with 20 employees or less—who were least likely to be able to afford custom forms from traditional forms providers, who typically produced customized forms in very long runs suited for larger organizations.

To get his business going, Anderson moved to Townsend, Massachusetts, assembling a selection of business forms which he had produced by various printing firms. He began mailing brochures to promote his new offering. His sense of the market need and good potential return on investment played out well. By 1955, he had moved out of his barn into office space, and he brought Jay R. Rhoads, Jr., on board to help handle the business side of his growing custom forms business. By 1968, NEBS posted $3.5 million in net sales. The 90,000 active customers for its products were serviced by 163 full- and part-time employees.[1]

In 1970, Anderson retired and Rhoads and his brother, Richard H. Rhoads, took over the business, setting out to put it on a growth path. Richard was

---

1   Source: Hoovers.com

still Chairman when I came on board in 1993. Key to their growth at the time was the ability to handle a large volume of small orders quickly (usually with a six-day turnaround), and soon 70 percent of the company's business consisted of reorders from satisfied customers who enjoyed the service level and convenience that NEBS offered. By 1973, the brothers had enough volume to justify bringing manufacturing in-house in order to eliminate dependence on outside printers. This move improved both margins and operational control for the company.

The company went public in 1977. By that time, it was international in scope, offering services in the United States and English-speaking Canada. As the 1980s dawned, NEBS had established a call center, and nearly half of its orders were coming in via phone. In 1985, the company launched its first bilingual forms to better serve the Canadian market.

By the time I joined the company as CEO, NEBS supported about two and a half million very small customers with call center operations, mail order services, and some vertical specialization, including the One-Write manual check writing system to support very small business accounting requirements of the time. At the time, though the company was financially strong, it had stagnated. The company's revenue growth had been stalled for the previous four years; the company badly needed a shot of innovation. We were able to provide that by applying the principles of Pragmatic Innovation.

Getting Started with NEBS

Five years prior to joining NEBS as the CEO, based on a recommendation of then IBM CEO John Akers, NEBS—an IBM customer—requested that I join the Board of Directors of its growing small business to provide them with an understanding and perspective relative to the new technologies that were affecting their business model. This was a great opportunity to truly understand how technology was impacting smaller businesses and again speaks to the importance of executives spending time outside of their comfortable cocoons to measure the effectiveness of potential products and technologies in the real-world marketplace. A real-world versus theoretical view based on a fresh view of the market is always helpful to any top executive.

It was clear to me that as computing became more prevalent in smaller businesses, NEBS could be an early market entrant to support the need for computer forms. Pin-fed continuous forms designed to be printed on dot matrix printers became a growing business segment for the company.

NEBS had been a long-time IBM customer, using IBM mini-computers to run its business, starting with the System/32, graduating progressively to the System/36, System/38, and the AS-400.

Although the proliferation of computers had been a growth driver for NEBS, as the 1990s began to unfold, the increasing proliferation of desktop publishing, driven in large part by the IBM PC I brought to market, began to eat away at market share. Small businesses now had tools in place to create their own forms, stationery and signage. The manual check writing system was on its way to obsolescence as PC-compatible accounting software such as Quicken and PeachTree began to gain popularity.

Although NEBS continued to introduce new products to the market, the forms market was in decline due to all of these dynamics. In 1993, the company's 2,217 employees were able to serve the needs of more than 1.2 million small business customers with a 48-hour turnaround time. But earnings and revenue showed a different picture. In 1990, NEBS reported net income of $20.6 million; only two years later it would see that figure shrink to $15.47 million. By 1993, net income reached a record low: $14.2 million on sales of $237.1 million.

So already having an understanding of the technologies, the marketplace, and the executive management team, as well as the issues surrounding this company, I accepted the challenge of becoming the CEO and found myself bringing Pragmatic Innovation to this quarter billion dollar company then based in Groton, Massachusetts.

Moving Beyond Commodity

On the surface, the forms industry seems like the ultimate in commodity sales. Forms are generally utilitarian; people do depend on them for collecting and organizing business information. But forms are not generally top of mind for most business people, especially at an executive level. At NEBS, through the application of the Pragmatic Innovation process, we thought we could change our position by introducing features, functionality, and services that moved forms beyond the commodity zone. Along the way, we found an entirely new market for the company that was underserved by us and by others. That discovery, among others, led to some significant business growth for NEBS. It also positioned the company to be acquired, based on our having achieved our mission of creating a company whose products and services were positioned in a more attractive and efficient way to enhance its revenue growth. NEBS products and services migrated from a product offering to solutions that helped small businesses manage, promote and grow *their* businesses.

At the time I joined the company, small retail was the company's largest niche, and products had been expanded beyond forms to include bags, tags, stationery, signage, check writing systems, and more, all products this market segment needed to run their businesses. The demand for new forms was also growing, largely due to increased government regulatory activity for small businesses supported by, of course, forms.

Today, NEBS—as a division of Deluxe—is on a growth path, supplying products and services to more than six million small businesses and home offices across North America. Its product offerings include checks, business forms, envelopes, labels, greeting cards, merchandising aids, advertising specialties, promotional apparel, embossed foil anniversary seals, stationery, and packaging, shipping and warehouse supplies—all designed and priced to meet the needs of small businesses. NEBS also provides payroll services to small businesses in Canada.

Implementing Pragmatic Innovation at NEBS

Almost immediately, I gained the agreement of the Board and executive management to establish a team to do a thorough strategy review as the first step in an effective Pragmatic Innovation implementation. In order to know where you are going, you must fully understand where you are. It had been some time since the company had taken the time to holistically assess its positioning, messaging, and offerings.

I assigned our young and energetic corporate general counsel, Mike Dowd, who was also a good communicator, to lead the team. Our HR executive, Peter Zarilla, was also an integral part of this early effort. Both executives were well-respected by the Board and other managers at the company. We selected representatives from each of the functions in the organization to serve on this strategic task force. To begin the process, Mike and I interviewed each of the executives and members of the strategy team. We then presented what we had learned to the executive and strategy teams in our first interactive SWOT analysis. This ended up being a relatively quick process at NEBS.

As a result of reviewing and adding to early findings during the SWOT analysis, we discovered that we had not been following developments in the very small business (VSB) market closely enough. We were not up to date on the needs and requirements of this dynamic market segment. We put work assignments in place, the most important one being dispatching a group to find out who was opening all of these new VSBs and why they were not buying from NEBS. In addition, we made the following assignments to round out the research process:

- Perform benchmarking studies on other call center operations
- Review all products to determine performance parameters
- Review competitive activities
- Look at sales by region of the company
- Look at potential acquisitions
- Review software business issues
- Look at alternative distribution systems
- Review competitiveness of our manufacturing process
- Review our position on NASDAQ

As we regrouped to review findings, one of our most startling discoveries was that a large number of the new VSB's were now being started by women, primarily offering professional services. We talked with the Small Business Bureau and interviewed a number of new, small start-ups to learn more about their requirements. We learned that these woman-owned VSBs were buying forms and stationery primarily from local printers. By working with a local printer, they were able to add color and personalization to their forms and business stationery to differentiate themselves and promote their businesses. Color had become more important in the marketplace, largely due to a gender shift and the necessity to differentiate these new businesses. This was a marked change from the previous decades that were satisfied with monochromatic products.

At that point in time, NEBS did not offer custom color printing. This finding suggested a new business opportunity that we felt we could leverage to stimulate growth. By making acquisition of custom color forms and business stationery easier than traveling to the local commercial printer, and more cost effective as well, we believed we could attract these new customers to our services. NEBS had built its reputation on its fast turnaround and convenient access at a very competitive price. We believed those attributes would be important to this market. We had already proven that once we gained customers, we tended to keep them. This high level of customer retention generated a healthy annuity revenue stream for the company.

In line with another step in the Pragmatic Innovation process, we then asked the team to create a realistic business plan to address the custom color printing market. Their recommendations included:

- Bringing in communications experts to create a marketing plan for the new approach

- Developing a new product line based on custom color printing, specifically targeted at woman-owned VSBs

- Developing a new custom color catalog

- Developing short run printing techniques that supported color fidelity standards, initially in our New Hampshire plant, but with a plan to extend this offering to other plants for better geographic distribution of our production efforts

We called the program *Company Colors,* and it was later rebranded as NEBS Colors. In addition, we tested a new sales channel, creating a pilot arrangement with Kinko's (now FedEx Kinko's, recently rebranded to FedEx Office) to set up kiosks in selected stores. We wanted to test the effect that bringing our point of sale closer to new VSB's would have on adoption rates.

The team made other recommendations about the business as well. As a result, we did a number of things to streamline and revitalize NEBS, including:

- We reviewed all of the SKUs in the NEBS product line for line-item profitability and their relative importance in maintaining customer satisfaction. As a result of this review, we were able to eliminate 30 percent of our SKUs without any measurable negative impact on revenues.

- We began to strengthen our call center coverage by benchmarking leaders in this field with visits to companies who were considered the best at that time. This included companies like insurance firm USAA in Houston, Texas.

- We recommended the addition of a desktop publishing solution to the product portfolio to leverage the booming PC business. This program was ultimately launched as Page Magic, and was accompanied by a line of coordinating paper products.

- We recommended the development of a Windows version of One-Write Plus, a DOS application that had been developed to carry on the tradition established by our One-Write manual check writing system to take advantage of the emergence of a wide variety of desktop accounting packages.

- We added more software expertise to our call centers to improve our toll-free support system for the Page Magic and One-Write Plus software business. [2]

- We set up an operation in Phoenix that was focused on color development in an attempt to extend our business to the West Coast.

---

2   Eventually, this software business was sold to PeachTree Software, who was in a much better position to provide software support. Since this was not a core business for us, we were never able to develop the appropriate organizational synergies to be able to deliver software support in a cost-effective manner, and it was eating us alive with support costs.

Based on the low volume of performance by our market makers on NASDAQ, we also decided to switch our stock to the New York Stock Exchange to see whether we could get more focus and activity-driven trading there.

Some of these recommendations were deployed by our international operations as well. Our Canadian operation picked up the Kinko's idea by establishing a similar arrangement with Mail Boxes, Etc. of Canada. We also leveraged many of these ideas to bolster our UK operation.

When Pragmatic Innovation begins to drive new initiatives, it can have tremendous communication value to investors and customers. This was the case with our 1995 NEBS Annual Report. This report dedicated its Business Highlights section to these newly emerging innovations and developments, citing them as major accomplishments, with the following statements:

- **Kinko's Alliance**. One of the more promising developments during the year was the formation of an alliance with Kinko's, Inc. Through the alliance, the Company's design and printing services were made available to small businesses at select sites within Kinko's network of more than 750 retail stores. At fiscal year end, the Company had established 22 custom print desks in Kinko's stores and announced a joint commitment with Kinko's to grow the number to a minimum of 50 stores by December 1995. The alliance provides Kinko's with access by mail to millions of small businesses, while the Company gains direct access to the $10 billion retail market for small business printing services.

- **Company Colors**. The Company's new image-building line was created in response to customer demand for printed products combining functionality with coordinated color and design. Company Colors offers a full range of manual and computer forms, business cards, stationery, and related products in five popular two-color combinations with consistent design elements.

- **Software Products**. Page Magic desktop publishing software and its companion line of laser printer papers were introduced through direct mail and retail in the second fiscal quarter. The Company's market-leading One-Write Plus accounting package continued to exhibit strong sales through mail order. Development of a Windows version of One-Write Plus progressed throughout the year with introduction expected during fiscal 1996. The Company has continued to invest heavily in the development of One-Write Plus for Windows and to establish cost-effective technical support.[3]

- **International Operations**. The Company's Canadian subsidiary exhibited renewed strength and posted its best performance in several years. The improvement was led by new products, improved marketing programs, and the improving Canadian economy. In a promising venture, the Canadian subsidiary arranged to display the Company's products in self-service kiosks in selected Mail Boxes, Etc. of Canada stores. Revenues generated by the Company's UK branch also exhibited renewed growth driven by product and market initiatives.

The Results

In a mere 15 months after establishing our Pragmatic Innovation task force, NEBS saw a significant increase in revenue and profit following four

---

3   As I indicated, the ultimate inability to develop cost-effective technical support led us to selling off this business. But the improvements we made, plus the Windows development strategy, positioned it well for the sale.

years of stagnation. Much of the credit for the financial turnaround was accredited to the introduction of the *Company Colors* forms and stationery business targeted at woman-owned VSBs that our team had developed using the principles of Pragmatic Innovation.

In recognition of this turnaround, our stock price continually crept up from $15 per share, where it had languished for some time, to more than $23 per share. This tremendous investor value in a relatively short period of time was driven by the proper implementation and execution of the Pragmatic Innovation process in this smaller company. It blended a new market understanding with a renewed spirit of innovation to revitalize the organization.

The benefits did not stop there. From its initial modest beginnings in 1993, the *Company Colors* program was expanded and formally relaunched with new branding in early 1996 under the name NEBS Colors. A testimonial to its success was the following statement, which appeared in the 1996 NEBS annual report:

> NEBS Colors, one of the most successful product introductions in NEBS history, was unveiled in 1996. Unique in the direct mail industry, NEBS Colors offers small business a choice of color, type style, and contemporary design across a variety of manual and computer business forms. In response to today's more image-conscious consumer, NEBS Colors enables a small business to achieve a consistent, color-coordinated look across printed products without the expense of custom printing.

Pragmatic Innovation: The Benefits Are Clear

By the end of the NEBS experience, I was beginning to feel very comfortable with the Pragmatic Innovation process, although we still had not given it a name at that time. With IBM, Xerox, and Gulfstream, the process had evolved, gaining a higher level of functionality with each subsequent application. NEBS was the first instance where I could really see the impact of the process from beginning to end, with business results improving almost immediately. I began to see this process as a new breakout business strategy and as a result laid out a documented, step-by-step implementation strategy that I would take to several of the next businesses I became a part of in the following years.

As I reflect on what drove the success of the innovation at NEBS and previous companies, there were certain key steps that emerged as both telling and critical. Specifically:

- We had an executive sponsor—myself, in the key CEO role at Gulfstream and NEBS.

- We involved the executive team, careful not to let them overpower our activities by applying competing strategies that had delivered success for them in the past.

- We collected internal information and assigned an effective, well regarded, intelligent strategy leader who had good communication skills.

- We conducted a professionally-facilitated off-site SWOT analysis that led to the development of a preliminary business plan and uncovered opportunities for operational improvement.

- We looked externally to gain more information and proceeded to pursue our newly defined opportunities.

- We kept the Board involved every step of the way.

- Once this work was completed, we brought the team together every six to nine months to refresh our information, check our progress, and adjust our direction and/or add new initiatives. This step makes Pragmatic Innovation a closed-loop process that infuses innovation into the organization and prevents it from being a one-time, standalone event.

- Most importantly, we accomplished our business objectives.

The Pragmatic Innovation template was now gaining a more refined definition. Chapter Eight of this book offers a precise and focused summary of the Pragmatic Innovation process with actionable steps that any business can apply in order to infuse an innovative spirit into the organization. But my personal experiences at a few other organizations since leaving NEBS are also relevant to the discussion, add experiential learning and bear discussing, which I will do in the next chapter.

It is also important to reiterate that as a result of many of these initiatives conducted under my leadership, NEBS continued down a strong strategic path after my departure and was ultimately acquired by Deluxe Corporation. I believe its attractiveness as an acquisition target had much to do with the new strategies we developed as a result of our Pragmatic Innovation work. I also believe that without that work, NEBS would have continued to stagnate by pursuing a declining market without the benefit of the insight that Pragmatic Innovation delivers.

CHAPTER 6

Moore ... or Less

"Behold the turtle. He only makes progress when he sticks his neck out."

James Bryant Conant (1893 - 1978)

American chemist and university president

... And PROAMICS (a start-up)

When you work with as many companies as I have and are as familiar with as many leaders in American industry as I am, you gain a unique perspective on what truly makes innovation work ... and you also learn what can doom an innovation strategy. I saw this latter case first-hand during my business experience with

Moore Corporation, where lack of leadership and focus at the top prevented any sustainable innovation from taking place.

In the fall of 1995, I received a phone call from the CEO of Moore Corporation, Reto Braun, asking me if I had an interest in discussing a potential new assignment at Moore. I had met Reto when I was at Xerox Corporation while doing some joint work at Unisys. At that time, Reto was President and COO of Unisys.

Reto was a native of Switzerland, had been employed for a brief period with IBM in Europe, and then joined Unisys. He became President and CEO of Moore Corporation in 1993. At the time I met with Reto in 1995, Moore Corporation was recovering from an unsuccessful bid to take over competitor Wallace Computer Services, Inc., a hostile bid that was Reto's brainchild. This made front-page news, including Reto's boasting that there was no question Wallace's shareholders would find the Moore hostile bid compelling. In the end, Wallace shareholders rejected the bid in a very public move, and Reto's attempt drew fire from the industry at large as well. At the time, Moore stood at about $3 billion in annual revenues and had been under margin pressure in a declining forms industry.

Reto then determined that Moore was ready for a new strategic direction, and that he needed assistance with this effort. That is where I came in. In addition, he still had not given up hope of acquiring Wallace at some time in the future, and he knew he needed to gain a deeper understanding of its internal workings and its technology in order to ultimately undertake a successful integration of the two companies. Among other things, he was aware that Wallace had more aggressively invested in modern information systems than Moore had. That allowed the company to drive higher value products and services into the customer base.

A Bit of Background

Moore's manufacturing plants had grown up autonomously and as a result had no real and consistent standards of operation across the enterprise. In a sprawling manufacturing operation like that of Moore in the mid-1990s, standardization would have been a huge benefit. Without it, for example, it was virtually impossible to close a plant to adjust the footprint to a declining market. Without standards, it was a challenge to move work from one plant to another. Closing a plant without the ability to offload its work in a streamlined fashion was a recipe for disaster. But so was keeping an underutilized plant open—a Catch 22 if there ever was one.

Moore's information systems were also aged. Legacy systems had inconsistencies from one segment of the business to another and integration efforts, had there been any underway, would have presented a serious and very expensive challenge.

While there was some effort within the company to enter new, higher value technology-based businesses, these efforts were relatively small. The vast majority of the executive team had grown up in the forms business—much like Xerox's team growing up in the copier business—and they were much more comfortable dealing with the legacy business than they were in dealing with the actions required to grow the company into new markets.

Setting Pragmatic Innovation in Play at Moore

At Reto's behest, then, I joined Moore Corporation as Executive Vice President in charge of North American Operations early in 1996. He was still focused on acquiring Wallace and believed that my past experiences could be put to use. Without the Wallace acquisition, he felt, I might be able to help Moore generate new opportunities in the North American market, which comprised about 70 percent of the business. Either way, he felt I could contribute to the organization. Either way, I believed that undertaking a Pragmatic Innovation initiative was critical to developing new opportunities.

We began in earnest to develop a plan that would allow the company to consolidate manufacturing, build a new, more flexible information systems infrastructure, and bring in new growth opportunities compatible with the business that would take advantage of existing strong customer relationships. As part of the engagement terms, I told Reto that I would be bringing in some outside resources that would accomplish two things: 1) beef up the skill sets within my new organization; and 2) infuse new blood, new experiences and new capabilities into the team of experienced people Moore already had in place.

Some of the new people I recruited included Tim Cunningham in Finance, Mark Wieshaar in Business Development, Diana Munro in Marketing, Sieg Buck in operations, and Chuck Buchheit in software application development. I had worked with many of these people before, primarily at Xerox, and I had strong confidence in their ability to help us make the next strategic leap at Moore.

With the team in place, I began to unfold the Pragmatic Innovation approach, which was now fairly clear in my mind as a replicable and effective process. As with previous engagements, we initiated our innovation efforts by launching a comprehensive SWOT analysis. This coupled Moore's paradigm and view of the marketplace with the expertise and recent outside perspective of some of the new members of the management team, resulting in a fresh view of the opportunities—and threats—before us. The team had several off-site meetings and within six months had completed a comprehensive situation analysis.

Some of Moore's key strengths that were highlighted as a result of this work included its strong label product knowledge, effective market positioning in certain key verticals, and a strong customer base with high levels of customer satisfaction. At the same time, we identified weaknesses in our performance ratios, a declining market share in key areas, and total dependence on a declining forms market as a key business growth driver. We also discovered that the company had no global marketing view and was suffering from other problems as a result of the existing bureaucratic business structure.

The primary recommendation that came out of this work was that Moore Corporation needed to transform itself from an exclusive manufacturing focus to a company that viewed services, technology, integrated solutions, and solutions with differentiated technology as part of its future vision. This, we believed, was necessary in order for the company to succeed in the coming years. Our new strategic plan envisioned efforts to pursue growth markets such as Brazil, China, and some other Asian markets. It also envisioned the divestiture of non-strategic businesses such as Toppan Moore Equity, Inforite, and Sabre. We further recognized the need for certain strategic alliances and partnerships with companies such as EDS, Adobe, IBM, Netscape, and NEPS, a small but quite successful company that I had worked with over a number of years. Moore ultimately acquired NEPS and made it the company's Emerging Technologies Division. We believed that by virtue of its well-established, innovative and successful software solutions, NEPS could drive higher value print volume in our current large accounts, and that supposition proved out.

In addition, we identified various data centric opportunities which we believed could drive higher margin business growth for Moore. These included print-on-demand marketing services for large manufacturing companies and an entry into the variable print market.

We also saw some immediate opportunities for standardization which we believed could be deployed across the organization. These efforts would lead to redeployment and consolidation of some existing manufacturing capabilities.

We identified strategic investments and laid out an investment plan that included an analysis of growth and margin potential. As part of our work, we also explored the acquisition of my alma mater NEBS, but that did not pan out for various reasons. Another outgrowth of my time at NEBS came closer to happening, and that was the potential acquisition of Kinko's.

Keeping in Touch with Kinko

Paul Orfalea [pronounced OR'-Fah-La] founded Kinko's in 1970 near the University of California at Santa Barbara with a simple idea: provide college students with products and services they need at a competitive price. The space that Orfalea rented for his copy business was so small the copy machine was used out on the sidewalk. From its modest beginnings, Kinko's has grown to an industry icon, and now as a part of Federal Express, appears to be on a path of reinventing itself yet again.

I'm sure you have heard the story: as Orfalea and his pals were determining what they should call their new business, Orfalea's nickname—Kinko, after his curly hair—was selected. As of this writing, Orfalea still holds an honorary role with FedEx Kinko's as Chairman Emeritus while also teaching at the University level and pursuing philanthropic efforts through his Foundation, a private nonprofit organization serving the personal choices of the Orfalea family. It supports high quality, preventative and experiential community programs which directly impact children, youth, and underprivileged families of Santa Barbara, Ventura and San Luis Obispo Counties.

Paul and I got to know each other when we worked through the distribution strategy for NEBS, and we have stayed in touch over the ensuing years.

Looking back to the mid-1990s, Kinko's was comprised of 125 partnerships. The partners, in general, had come to the organization at a fairly young age. By this time, many were in their mid-40s and a large number of them were ready to cash out and move on to other things. Paul called to talk to me, since he had come to the conclusion he needed to sell the company.

At Paul's invitation, I met with Kinko's Partners' Committee to begin due diligence. As a result of our investigations, the acquisition of Kinko's appeared to be aligned with some of the new strategies we wanted to deploy as part of innovation at Moore. I took the concept to Moore's Board, touting it as an opportunity that could really change the way we operated.

Ultimately, Moore was willing to purchase Kinko's. But when Paul took the proposal to the Partners' Committee, the group decided they would rather pursue an IPO. At the time, of course, IPOs were hot, and there were lots of get-rich-quick stories going around.

Kinko's ultimately chose Clayton Dubiliere to take the company public. During the process, Paul was pushed aside. He was the spiritual and charismatic leader of the organization, but since that time, he has certainly done a terrific job of moving on with his life and is making very valuable contributions.

Although it took longer than anyone expected, I am sure, Kinko's was ultimately acquired by FedEx became FedEx Kinko's, and now the Kinko's name has been dropped with the division being known as FedEx Office.

Hindsight Is a Wonderful Thing

During this initial effort at Moore, we used a modified version of the Pragmatic Innovation process. We undertook all or most of the steps I have previously identified, but there was one key element missing. Although the management team enthusiastically exerted incredible energies and effort during the process, in hindsight, I now understand that we did not have the required corporate sponsor to drive innovation through the organization. We did not truly have Reto's buy-in. Without the support of the CEO—whose focus remained on acquisition—innovation did not have an opportunity to truly succeed. I quickly found out how serious that mistake was.

Making the Tough Choices

In the summer of 1997, Reto invited me to present our strategy work to Moore's Board of Directors at the Toronto office. After our presentation, Reto then submitted a separate strategic proposal to make another run at Wallace. He had also invited an outside consulting group that had been working with him on developing a revamped Wallace take-over strategy. I began to see that Reto was obsessed with acquiring Wallace, even to the overall detriment of Moore's financial health.

With two proposals before the Board, Reto stated that he would prefer to pursue acquisition rather than innovation. But to my surprise, he asked Board members to determine which of the two proposals they would prefer to pursue.

Reto's question created a very lively discussion and debate amongst the Board members and the Executive management team, as one could imagine. At the end of the process, though, the Board's direction was clear: Pursue the innovation strategy that I had presented. Though I was pleased with the Board's decision, it remained unclear to me and others on the innovation team how we could be successful with this effort without Reto's support.

The following week, Reto made it clear what his perspective was. He announced to me and several of the executive team members that he had absolutely no interest in pursuing our innovation plan, regardless of what the Board had decided. His rationale was that he had pursued these types of growth strategies when he first came to Moore, and he was not willing to go through such an effort again. He was thoroughly convinced that the only path forward for business growth was acquisition. With that mindset, I still do not understand to this day why he allowed an alternate plan to be submitted to the Board. Perhaps he truly believed that the Board would see things his way, and he was only humoring us in recognition of all of the effort we had invested in the process. Within several weeks of the Board meeting, Reto began to dismantle the organization I had assembled and released some of the key new hires I had made.

I subsequently left Moore Corporation. I had come to Moore with the hope and belief that a Pragmatic Innovation approach could truly work. But I had underestimated Reto. Reto, in turn, underestimated his Board. Two months later, the Board of Directors asked Reto Braun to resign.

Ultimately, of course, Moore did acquire Wallace and the combined entity was then snapped up by RR Donnelley—already the largest printer in the world, but raising itself to the $9 billion mark in annual revenues with this large acquisition. The combined company has made some acquisitions to diversify, but has primarily remained focused on continued industry consolidation.

Reflections on Moore

Reflecting on this experience, it certainly reinforces that a no-nonsense Pragmatic Innovation approach cannot be undertaken in a vacuum. It must begin with full support and approval from the top. To change an organization and to instill creativity, entrepreneurship, and the development of innovative ideas, the ultimate responsibility begins and ends there.

The most important thing I learned from the experience was that certain companies and their executives have within their culture and their DNA the ability to incubate new strategic thinking—or not. Frank Carey had it. David Kearns had it. Richard Rhoads had it, to some extent.

Even when a collective team of new and dynamic thinkers are encouraged to employ these disciplined practices, unleashing new information that creates tremendous strategic value, you can not dictate change from the middle of the organization. The desire or intention to bring innovation to fruition must be driven from the top. This was an important, but somewhat costly, learning for me, and I took it to heart as I moved on to other opportunities. It was one I would certainly not overlook again!

On to Proamics

Meanwhile, as a result of the Moore experience, Cristina and I and our family had settled in Lake Forest, Illinois. We enjoyed the community and our lifestyle, and we had no desire to relocate again. So I set about looking for the next opportunity, one that would allow us to remain in Lake Forest.

That opportunity arose with a small ($10 million in annual revenues) software company headquartered in our community. While this is a significantly smaller engagement than those I had been involved with in the past and would be involved with in the future, it is important to share this experience as a demonstration of the fact that Pragmatic Innovation works in all sizes and types of organizations. All organizations, regardless of size or number of products, can find ways to broaden their strategic view and focus with this process.

Another reason for becoming involved with Proamics is that I have always enjoyed technology, and this offered me the opportunity to become involved in a company with some great technology.

I joined the company as an external consultant to help them develop a break-out strategy. Proamics was founded by three partners: Malcolm Lotzoff, Drew Van Voren and Rich Hawkinson. They had a satisfied customer base that they supported with project management software for service-oriented companies. They had been running at break-even levels for some time, and were looking to take the company to the next level.

At Proamics, we used an abbreviated and accelerated Pragmatic Innovation process that included a SWOT analysis involving the entire management team. In this case, we had full and wholehearted support from top management. That was one mistake I wouldn't make again!

During the data-gathering process, we spoke with customers, suppliers, business partners, and distributors. We identified some immediate actionable efforts, including new requirements in documentation, some product enhancements, and additional activities involving distribution, service and support, and marketing. We also raised some additional capital for the firm from Vector Capital of San Francisco.

This was clearly a success story. Within six months of implementing these actions, Proamics had raised $13 million in capital, and within a year had profitably doubled its revenues to $20 million. The investors, recognizing the exploding growth the company was achieving, arranged meetings with a Goldman Sachs backed firm to explore acquisition opportunities. Proamics was acquired by NIKU. The company went public in early 2000.

Proamics was an example of how quickly a full Pragmatic Innovation process can be deployed and how quickly it can deliver measurable benefits. Of course, a smaller organization allows for all the key management to be much more involved in the process than is possible in a very large organization. By doing so, management is able to gain a deeper understanding of the value and relevance of Pragmatic Innovation in the development of a break-out strategy. They would tell you that without Pragmatic Innovation, they would likely still be lingering in the sub-$20 million range. As a result of this positive experience, senior managers are more likely to ensure that innovation is engrained into the DNA of the company.

Following Proamics, I have continued my work with many entrepreneurial firms over recent years, including my role at another $10 million firm based in New Hampshire, NEPS, where I served as CEO for a time. NEPS promises to be a true showcase for Pragmatic Innovation, as you will see later in the book. Although it is still a work in progress as I write this, it embodies all of my learnings over the past two-plus decades and had the added advantage of having a strong, and very innovative leader in the person of its founder, Denise Miano, who was willing to play a different role in the organization in order to give it the best opportunity to grow.

The DNA of Innovation

I recently read an article in U.S. News and World Report about a consultant who advises companies on innovation. He suggested that what our country needs is an "Innovation President." He believes this is essential to bring about the necessary change in business and education that is required to ensure that America remains on the cutting edge in innovation. This reminded me of an amazing moment in U.S. history that I referenced in Chapter One—when

President John F. Kennedy challenged American scientists in education and in industry to work together to ensure that America was the first country to send a man to the moon. Perhaps Kennedy was an early example of an Innovation President. His challenge certainly drove the country to achieve dramatic innovation across a wide swath of disciplines. It is perhaps the most dramatic example in our history of the role vision, leadership, and throwing down the gauntlet can play in reaching magnificent achievements.

I strongly believe that innovation is critical to the future of our country and its citizens. The stories in this book are just a few examples—the ones I happened to have personal experience with—but they offer tremendous testimony as to what is possible. As you read through the remainder of this book, I hope you will agree with me that it is important for us as business, educational and political leaders to challenge our innovative capabilities. By imbuing our national culture with innovation down to its very DNA—or as some would say, to allow us to recapture the innovative spirit that led to our strength on the world playing field in the first place—we position ourselves to compete effectively in today's dynamic global economy. We can always hope that we end up with an Innovation President that might speed our progress along, much as John Kennedy did with his space challenge. But as leaders, we can also make sure that innovation is inherent within our respective spheres of influence, and that is what I have dedicated the balance of my life to doing.

Now, a very brief summary of the rest of the book

In the remaining three chapters, I will outline how Pragmatic Innovation is impacting the future of NEPS. Chapter Eight is designed be used as a reference by anyone attempting to launch their own Pragmatic Innovation

Program. In the final chapter, I will talk about how I have come full circle to work with IBM again in an effort designed to solve the problem of how to deliver innovative, cost-effective technology that will deliver the information available on the Internet into the classroom.

CHAPTER 7

NEPS

—*The Next Generation of Customer Communications*

"I like thinking big...
if you're going to be thinking anyway, you might as well think big."

DONALD TRUMP (1946 -) AMERICAN REAL ESTATE DEVELOPER

ow is an appropriate time to refer back to my discussion about Ted Nelson in Chapter One. I firmly believe that the way you can judge the viability of new ventures in the

technology industry is to determine whether they are making a contribution that furthers the ubiquity and convergence of communications and computer technology. Ted Nelson understood that in the 1970s when he said computer technology was moving in the direction of "*making all information available to all people, no matter who they were, or when, where and how they wanted it.*" His visionary outlook has proven to be true, and technology has extended those capabilities farther than even he probably was able to foresee. But there is still much to be done.

This belief has been reinforced for me over and over again. Both the IBM PC and the Xerox DocuTech advanced this cause. Just think about the products that have come from Apple that also further this objective. Look at the results Apple has achieved from them and the changes Apple's innovations have driven into the marketplace and society as a whole—the Macintosh, the iPOD and the iPhone, to name a few. On the PC side, personal computers have become more flexible and more portable, and are capable of being connected from anywhere, going far beyond what we ever dreamed was possible when we launched the first IBM PC in 1981. Add to that satellite communications, cell phones, PDAs, and the myriad of other communications devices we have available to us—and that we will see coming our way in the future.

There is no question that there is a glut of information and technology, but there is an increasing array of knowledge management tools of various types to help us sort through what is important and what is not. There is some terrific software that allows us to integrate database information, on-demand printing, and computer and communications technology to spawn a whole new era of customer communications and promotions geared to delivering the right messages at the right time via the right medium to the right individual recipients for maximum communications effectiveness.

I became engaged with NEPS because I believe the company and its partners have the technology and solutions that will enable them to be as big a play in their realm of customer communications solutions as the PC and the DocuTech were in the realms of technology and printing. What we NEPS is bringing to market will certainly be more important than the Gulfstream GV in the overall scope of human development.

As I look back over the various ventures I have been involved in, I find it interesting that there is a sort of convergence of those achievements in the work we are doing today at NEPS. I wish I could honestly say that I, like Ted Nelson, had the vision way back when to know where all of this was heading. I didn't. But as I pursued my career path, I was able to take the lessons learned from each engagement, continue to build on them and leverage them into this proven Pragmatic Innovation approach.

Taking a Clean-Sheet Approach

As I indicated, it was this line of thinking that got me interested in NEPS. I had gotten to know NEPS Founder Denise Miano back in the Xerox days when we were preparing to launch the DocuTech. She was the first to deliver a solution that connected DocuTech to the network, unleashing incredible power from a machine that was well ahead of its time even without this important connectivity. She has plenty of other firsts on her list of achievements.

Denise has more than twenty-five years of experience in systems design and the implementation of leading-edge document management and printing technologies. She cut her teeth in the demanding insurance industry and leveraged that knowledge to found NEPS in 1988. At the time, she recognized an emerging need in paper-intensive organizations like insurance companies for integrating and automating the document production lifecycle. She brought breakthrough thinking to the marketplace, and she has continued to be an innovator over the ensuing years.

At one point as I mentioned in Chapter Six, NEPS was acquired by Moore and became the company's Emerging Technologies Division. Being folded into a stodgy, older firm like Moore must have been quite a shock for Denise after being on her own for so long. It is a testament to her strength of character and the support of a few visionary executives at the company that she was able to continue to innovate there, not letting the organization drag her into any of the pitfalls Rosabeth Moss Kantor describes. Subsequent to Moore's acquisition by printing giant RR Donnelley, Denise negotiated a spin-out and took the company back.

Taking her company independent again was quite an achievement for Denise, especially since she was able to retain ownership of all of the relevant intellectual property she had brought with her into Moore as well as much of what was developed during the time her company was a division of Moore. But going back to an independent company was not without its trials and tribulations. In order to continue to grow, she needed to secure a funding source, and that is when we hooked up again. Cristina and I had been working with Hispania Capital Partners to help them find investments. When NEPS came to my attention, I knew it was well worth pursuing, especially because of my past experience in working with Denise, and because it was positioned squarely in the midst of the convergence of communications and computer technology.

So while NEPS was an "old" company—having been in business in one form or another for nearly 20 years—it was at the same time almost a start-up opportunity. We had a core staff of very talented people, we had great technology, and we had the ability to take a clean-sheet approach to the development of a go-forward strategy. That is exactly what we set out to do.

Beginning from a Position of Strength

NEPS has an amazing portfolio of human and technology resources, including several unique packaged products targeted primarily at the health care and financial services industries, as well as deep systems integration expertise that allows the company to compete effectively for business that requires customized document solutions in the content management and production management arenas.

Make Meaning

Apple Fellow and venture capitalist Guy Kawasaki has written a great deal about innovation and frequently speaks on the subject. He identifies a number of criteria for defining innovative products and services, among which are that they Make Meaning and facilitate Jumping to the Next Curve. He believes, as do I, that companies worthy of investment should bring to market things that can change the world, perpetuate and create good, and have an impact on ending or mitigating the bad. That is what he means by Making Meaning, pointing out that all too often, the primary driver for entrepreneurs is to make money, and saying, "If you make meaning, you will probably also make money. But if you start out to make money, you will attract the wrong kind of people—MBAs, investment bankers, the two worst kind of people to attract to a company that is trying to be innovative. The basis for all innovation is the desire to make meaning in life."[1]

By Jumping to the Next Curve, Kawasaki means that to qualify as innovative, the goal should not be a 10 percent improvement over an existing product or service, but rather, a 10X improvement. He draws heavily on examples, of course, from his alma mater, Apple, such as the Macintosh, which he helped bring to market, and the iPOD. I am fully confident that if Kawasaki looked at what NEPS is doing, he would agree that there is a huge amount of innovation that Jumps to the Next Curve.

---

1   Speech delivered at EFI Connect 2007, June 12, 2007, Las Vegas, Nevada (www.efi.com/connect2007)

Building the Competency Base

When I joined NEPS, we were beginning from a position of strength. But it was clear from the outset that there were some competencies we could add to the organization to make it stronger, most notably on the services side. With that in mind, one of the first things we did was work with Hispania Capital Partners to acquire another Boston-based, woman-owned firm, Art Plus Technology, Inc. (APT), the premier provider of document and information design services to the financial, insurance, and health care industries. APT was led by Liz Tindley, another capable and innovative female executive, and there were clear synergies between the two companies resulting in the sum of the parts being greater than the whole.

Also coincidentally founded in 1988, APT was far ahead of the curve in recognizing the value of using transactional documents, such as statements and invoices, as critical communications tools for more than simply transactional information. That concept is just beginning to gain traction in the market and is generally referred to as TransPromotional communications, or TransPromo, where marketing or educational messaging is integrated into the transactional document rather than being communicated using inserts or separate direct mail pieces. Combining the expertise of an information designer, a document systems integrator, and a management consulting firm in a single company, APT has revolutionized the document automation industry by providing a unified response to the challenges of the digital age. APT is not an advertising agency, but because corporate identity is such an important part of its document design work, the company does provide corporate identity guidelines for companies that do not already have them in place.

Like NEPS, APT has a heritage of innovation and a number of firsts to its credit, including:

- the first Microsoft Windows based report writer;

- the first high volume graphical investor statement;

- one of the earliest multi-language investor statements delivered in the United States.

TransPromotional Communications

Bills and statements are the one piece of mail you can be assured your customers will open and read every month. APT was ahead of the curve in recognizing that these often mundane documents can be very effectively leveraged as marketing tools, making them far more valuable than a normal utilitarian statement. By making the design more intuitive and adding color and customized informational messaging, bills and statements become easier to understand, and result in faster and more accurate payment and fewer calls to customer support centers. In addition, by placing targeted marketing messages on these statements, they can easily be converted from an operational expense—an accepted cost of doing business—to a revenue generator. Some enterprising companies are even selling space on their statements to related third parties to add value for their customers while generating an entirely new revenue stream for the company. These enhanced transactional documents are often called TransPromotional, or TransPromo, by industry pundits.

TransPromo is a hot area, with research firm InfoTrends projecting the North American market for TransPromo printed in full digital color will grow from 1.67 billion impressions in 2007 to 22.8 billion impressions by 2012. That is a 68 percent compound aggregate growth rate (CAGR)! APT was innovative enough to see this coming way ahead of the market, Making Meaning and Jumping to the Next Curve for its customers, bringing real value and innovation to their statements, invoices, and other transactional documents.

From a tactical perspective, APT provides services that encompass document design, document delivery, and the ability to reinvent and combine documents for more powerful communications. APT lives up to Ted Nelson's vision of developing *"a user interface ... so simple that a beginner in an emergency can understand it within ten seconds."* Although Ted wasn't referring to paper documents, the concept he was promoting could certainly be applied to these instruments which collect information and communicate it in a unique and innovative manner.

NEPS offers the rest of the picture—the underlying infrastructure required to produce those TransPromo communications. This includes content management, seamless linkages to a wide variety of enterprise and other databases, integration with corporate solutions such as SAP and Oracle, automated preparation of documents for delivery to a wide variety of printing devices and other communications media including email, text messaging and the Web, and the ability to manage the procurement of printed and electronic production and fulfillment services across the enterprise.

The combination of NEPS and APT has already started to pay off, with the award of a number of very high profile deals where our small company was competing against much larger companies. Augmenting our portfolio by combining these two innovative companies was the first step in putting Pragmatic Innovation to work.

Putting Pragmatic Innovation to Work

In a sense, the acquisition of APT was similar to the discussion I had at Xerox many years ago regarding being able to compete effectively with IBM Printing Systems. There are some things that are intuitive and very time sensitive, where you can't necessarily afford the time to work through the entire process. But it is equally critical to recognize that inevitably, you must work through the process in the bigger scheme of things. So even while all of the work toward completing the acquisition was going on, we were laying the Pragmatic Innovation groundwork to take NEPS to the next level.

Most importantly, as we began the process, we worked very hard to foster and protect the spirit of innovation in the combined companies.

One of the first challenges we had as a combined company was to distill our value proposition down to a concise statement that anyone could understand. With a set of services and capabilities as complex as we have, that can be easier said than done, and it will, of course, be a work in progress. But I was very happy with the initial "Who We Are" statement the team developed in support of our positioning as the leader in a new field of expertise we are calling Customer Communications Management.

We Orchestrate Information for Personalized, Individualized Delivery

- From any repository (financial, HR, CRM, etc.)
- Via any medium (paper, Web, email, etc.)
- For specific purposes (information sharing, brand reinforcement, cross-selling, etc.)

So you can create business communications that are simple, personal, clear, and effective

---

We tell people: If this is your challenge, we can help you. We do it by bridging the gap between the technology—that is, the capturing and management of information—and the solution, or the delivery of information, within a

Customer Communications context. This, in our opinion, has heretofore been the missing link in business communications. This model clearly Makes Meaning and Jumps to the Next Curve.

CUSTOMER COMMUNICATIONS MANAGEMENT: THE CRITICAL MISSING LINK

Capture	Content Management	**Communications Management**	Delivery
Obtaining the information to work with	Controlling and monitoring access to that information and the changes that are made to it	**Orchestrating the information for clear and effective, personalized delivery**	Presenting that information to the individual for whom it is intended

One early example of the power of this combined expertise was a deal NEPS ultimately won to support a provider of financial and insurance services to credit unions and their members. The financial services company initially sent out an RFP to 30 recipients to re-architect its platform for servicing policies, contracts and other transactional documents. The field was narrowed to five respondents based on responses to the RFP, with a final three being invited to give presentations. NEPS/APT ranked second in that narrowed field and did not initially get the deal, which went to a much larger company that offers a blend of printing and marketing services. However, it did not take long for the financial services company to realize that its first choice was not going to be able to deliver the goods, and the company came back to NEPS. Several months into implementation, they are extremely pleased with the results they are getting from the combined resources of NEPS and APT.

As we worked through the Pragmatic Innovation process, we performed a full Strengths-Weaknesses-Opportunities-Threats (SWOT) analysis of the combined companies. A summary of the SWOT input and the two-part SWOT questionnaire we used is included as an appendix to this book. It will serve as a good starting point for any company setting out to acquire the data that is required for a successful implementation of Pragmatic Innovation.

We did some market research to ensure that we had a broad view of the market. We conducted both formal and *ad hoc* discussions with our sales force, our customers, and our prospects. As a result of this work, we discovered that there was a huge, untapped market opportunity to develop a set of bundled services that could leverage our knowledge and expertise but bring these valuable Meaning-Making offerings to smaller organizations at an affordable price. This would allow smaller organizations to benefit from the same advanced level of Customer Communications Management Services that we have been able to deliver to our larger customers—something that has not previously been within the reach of smaller organizations. We call that new approach Fast2Market™. And we believe it is a breakthrough market approach that will go a long way toward taking NEPS and its customers to the next level. Fast2Market draws on the company's years of design experience to develop a starting point from which documents can be quickly and easily customized. It delivers:

- Rapid implementation of high-impact communications for organizations that lack the infrastructure, resources, and/or time for in-house deployment

- Design and hosting of policies, claims documents, applications, and marketing communications

- Lift out and conversion of legacy document management environments

- Secure, subscription access to leading technology

For example, a company may need to develop a new annuity statement. We determine what type of annuity statement they are looking for—equity indexed annuity, payout annuity, etc.—and draw from our full library of annuity statements to select just the one they need. These templates are already set up with all of the necessary regulatory language drawn from a database that we religiously keep current. They are set up to take a standard file feed generated by all of the major processors in the industry. They can be printed and/or presented electronically and then archived. The annuity package would also include related documents beyond the statement, such as transaction confirms and checks.

As far as I know, as of this writing, no one else is offering a breakthrough end-to-end packaged service like this. What would normally take many weeks of internal or consultant IT time to program legacy systems is reduced to a week or two. Clients retain strategic control and can focus on core competencies—i.e., developing new lines of business, and marketing and selling their products and services—while NEPS takes care of the management of the output process, including ensuring that all documents are compliant with ever-changing local, state and federal regulations.

As Liz is fond of saying, "We have done so many of these projects for large companies that we have implemented these documents in just about every possible way. If there is a way they can be presented, we have presented them that way."

The other benefit of having NEPS manage the whole process, especially for smaller companies or small lines of business within bigger companies, is that all of the production from a number of different companies is aggregated from a pricing perspective so that even the smallest companies can enjoy the same cost benefits their larger competitors are able to secure without the need to commit to large production volumes.

It is because of breakthrough solutions like Fast2Market that I believe NEPS will not stay small for long. That is why we have worked so hard, leveraging my years of Pragmatic Innovation experience, to ensure an environment at NEPS that fosters innovation and protects the key innovators that have made the successes possible.

As with other Pragmatic Innovation iniatives in which I have been involved, NEPS is constantly seeking a balance between protecting existing revenue streams to keep the company viable and rapidly deploying new concepts to the market to maintain a first-mover advantage. We don't ask, "Who else is doing it?" We ask, "What can we do that no one else is doing that will bring value to current and prospective customers?" We take things in small bites and look for replicable applications. We don't necessarily walk away from an innovative offering because it appears to be too small. That type of screening discourages innovative practices while encouraging step improvements in existing processes—and that is hardly innovative by anyone's definition. Not everything will work, but many things will. And by not waiting to find the next, giant killer app—the next iPOD or iPhone or IBM PC—we have been able to give birth to a plethora of innovative approaches that provide substantial benefit to us and our customers.

Making Pragmatic Innovation Work for You

As I write this chapter, it has only been a year since the Hispania funding for NEPS was closed and I took over as CEO. Much has been accomplished in a very short time, from the acquisition of APT to the acquisition of some very large, well-known customers over extremely stiff competition. We have made a good start in collecting data and leveraging that data into a concise strategy for the future. We have taken exceptional care of our innovators, nurturing their creativity and allowing them to work their magic with our customers, our employees and our offerings. It is now time for us to conduct a second level SWOT review and to create the next funding and growth plan to meet the next set of opportunities for NEPS. As is the case with a larger company, there are always those in the leadership team that hate to support a new direction. My biggest challenge, however, is with Hispania, the funding organization. This relatively small investor has a limited understanding of the business. Only time will tell whether they will grow with the company or allow the company to grow without them.

In many ways, it is too early to judge how successful NEPS will be. This success will require adding the next layer of experienced resources, both human and financial, and carefully selecting partners that can help NEPS achieve our potential. One of the best aspects of opportunities like NEPS is that this space will stay interesting and vital for some time to come.

Chapter Eight crystallizes the lessons I have learned over the years in the development of the Pragmatic Innovation process. It lays out a simple, repeatable process that has been proven to work in the more than 30 engagements in which it has been applied and during which it has been refined. While each application will necessarily differ to effectively address the size, industry, and cultural DNA of the organization, there is a consistent strategy that runs through all engagements that is required to ensure success.

CHAPTER 8

No-Nonsense Innovation —Getting Started

From the time I applied Pragmatic Innovation at IBM, to the ongoing work at NEPS, I have seen this process work, over and over again. I am convinced that it will bring value to any company who wholeheartedly embraces its precepts. In this chapter, I condense nearly 30 years of practice with Pragmatic Innovation into actionable steps that will guide you through the process.

At IBM, we employed Pragmatic Innovation across several organizations, including that responsible for development and launch of the PC. Frank Carey, the CEO, was the sponsor, and as I have stated many times, we could not have achieved what we did without his vision and leadership.

By the time I left IBM and joined Xerox, I was beginning to see a pattern, and set about employing the same principles there. Again, the CEO, David Kearns, was the champion. The time from initiation until we had a strategy in place was compressed as compared to IBM—about six months. And that timeframe has continued to compress as I have gained more experience with the process.

Of course, each organization is different, and some will, of necessity, take longer than others. It is also important to keep in mind that this is an evergreen process—it does not start and end like a project. Rather, when implemented properly, it is an evolving cultural change that can sustain innovation over time.

At Gulfstream, I was the sponsor as CEO, and it took the team three months to develop the plan we ultimately put in place. But Gulfstream also demonstrates one of the pitfalls. While Teddy Forstmann was supportive in the beginning, he did not have the patience required to change the business model and culture to allow innovation to flourish.

At NEBS, I was again the sponsor, and two to three months elapsed from the time we started until we had our initial plan in place. In all of these companies, the Board of Directors was heavily involved and provided the ultimate approval of our direction, with the exception of IBM, where it was the Corporate Management Committee.

At Moore, as I have related, we did develop plans and strategies that I believe would have made a difference and set a much different path for the company than ultimately occurred. But unfortunately, we were sabotaged by the CEO, who had a different agenda. This reinforced my commitment to gaining support from top leadership before proceeding with a program of Pragmatic Innovation. There are plenty of things to do in life without taking on projects that are destined to fail.

Proamics was the first implementation where I acted as a consultant, external to the organization, with full buy-in from the top. This experience allowed

me more free rein than I had had in the past, and freed me from the issues
that often arise when you are part of, or running, an organization. In a way,
it was a dispassionate, looking-in-from-outside experience that reinforced the
experience I had gather along the way and allowed me to refine them even more.
I have taken that experience, as a consultant, to nearly 30 additional companies.
At NEPS, I was in the CEO chair, working from the inside again. We have had
success with the process in as little as two weeks with small start-ups, although
the average tends to run two to three months for more established companies.

Across this broad spectrum of experiences, it is clear that Pragmatic
Innovation works, across industries and in various sizes of companies. It also
applies to companies that want to diversify as many product companies have
into related services. It is also clear that while some things will differ from
company to company, there is a consistent set of steps that must be followed
in order to deliver success. In Chapter One, we laid out ten success factors.
Those bear reviewing again before you get started.

But once you are ready to roll up your sleeves and get to work, these are
the practical steps that must be taken:

- Innovation Begins at the Top
- Innovation Needs a Change Agent
- Innovation is Open Minded and Cross-Functional
- Innovation Requires Collaboration
- Innovation Capitalizes on Internal Knowledge and
  External Perspective
- Innovation is Best When It Is Based on Data-Driven Analysis
- Innovation Can Benefit from Benchmarking
- Innovation Recommendations Should Be Prioritized and
  Consensus-Based
- Innovation Feeds on Continuous Improvement

Let's take a walk through each individually and in depth.

Innovation Begins at the Top

The Pragmatic Innovation process must begin with the full support of and a proactive stance on the part of the lead operating executive in the company. The IBM example shows how a visionary leader such as Frank Carey can overcome inertia and bureaucracy, allowing a skunk works such as the one we had in operation in Boca Raton, to flourish. David Kearns' leadership at Xerox was another great example. Once he was out of the picture and the organization was being led by Paul Allaire, it became more difficult to nurture the innovation and entrepreneurship that is necessary for success because Paul was really financially focused and was not comfortable leading decisions on strategy and product or service direction.

And in the most extreme case, Reto Braun literally sabotaged the effort. In that case, although we had developed some great ideas and strategies, not much was done in the way of implementation, and the effort quickly languished.

Executive leaders must have a strong desire to create new growth opportunities and a willingness to let trusted advisors or selected operational leaders collect information, reach out beyond current business practices, and challenge the status quo under their direction and leadership. Very often, the shedding of engrained practices and habits can be painful, almost like kicking the nicotine habit. We saw that happen at Xerox, where the management team, especially under Allaire's leadership, was comprised almost entirely of managers who had built successful careers on their ability to sell copiers. It was more than a decade, and several years into Anne Mulcahy's capable leadership, that Xerox began to make significant progress toward that end. The battle is ongoing, but there is light at the end of the tunnel.

The endeavor at Proamics was refreshing and rewarding because the culture was open to change and the leadership embraced the work we were about to undertake, as well as the strategies developed as a result of that work. The same was true of many of the other consulting engagements I undertook following that time. Perhaps part of the battle is won when the CEO makes a decision to make a significant investment in an outside resource. The company has some "skin in the game" and is more likely to persevere when things do not go as quickly or smoothly as one would like.

Insights

- The lead executive must desire a growth plan and be willing to sponsor the work to develop one, encouraging people to take a fresh look. This applies to service opportunities as well as new products and technology. It does not matter what the nature of the business is. Every type of business can benefit.

Innovation Needs a Change Agent

Pragmatic Innovation is about change, and not every change process leads to expected results. This is due to many factors, including unexpected changes in external conditions, or a lack of commitment and/or resistance to change from within the organization. Too many failed change projects, and employees can become disenchanted, unmotivated, and unwilling to try again. That is why it is important to seek a team leader who accepts the need for change and is capable of working in the organization to create an open, receptive environment. An effective change agent will have the confidence, intelligence and courage to challenge the status quo. An effective change agent must also have the flexibility to quickly detect and adjust to changes in internal and external conditions that have a bearing on the project.

This individual is likely to be a future leader in your organization and is generally selected from the mid-management ranks, rather than from the executive team. It should be someone who has the respect of the organization and who understands your business. Ideally, this change agent will have had significant experience in dealing with customers and a history of making decisions based on facts and data.

An alternative is to select an outside consultant who can lead the process, with the full support of the executive team.

Insights

- Be very thoughtful in selecting a change agent/team leader. This person is the most critical person in the process, once operating leadership is on board.

- Select a mid-level manager or executive within your organization who is familiar with your business, has experience with customers, and is used to dealing with and making decisions based upon facts and data. This change agent will shepherd the organization through the Pragmatic Innovation process, and must be respected by the organization while having the courage to challenge the status quo.

- If you employ an outside consultant, you will still need an internal leader. Ensure that your internal leader supports your choice and that the outside resource has real operational experience and a penchant for making data-based decisions.

Innovation is Open Minded and Cross-Functional

The best team is a cross-functional team comprised of operational managers from every segment of your business. They should have product- or customer-facing responsibilities and be drawn from one level below the direct reports to the CEO or COO. The reason for this is that—especially in larger businesses—direct reports have often been with the company for some period of time and are invested in the status quo and the decisions that have made them successful in the past. It is important to keep CEO/COO direct reports involved, but it is equally important to ensure that they do not quash new ideas prematurely.

Also consider adding one or more business managers—for example, from Finance—to the team to add business depth to the process.

In smaller organizations such as Proamics, the entire leadership team is generally intimately involved in the strategy process. The key consideration in smaller organizations, especially start-ups or companies where the founding entrepreneur still plays a leadership role, is to ensure that this individual does not overpower the process—something they are accustomed to doing and something that has likely contributed to their past successes.

Moving in new directions involves risk. Gathering information, both internally and externally, establishes a basis for understanding that risk prior to striking out on a new path. With that in mind, select team members who, like the team leader, have had experience in and a history of making decisions based on facts and data. Also, if the data points to issues, the story must be told, discussed, and reviewed with honesty, as painful as it is.

Based on overall resource availability, individual workloads and the time constraints you wish to place on the project, you should consider relieving team members of all or part of their day-to-day responsibilities. While this is not essential, or even desirable in some cases, it is worth considering in order not to overburden these valuable employees and to speed the process.

It is critical that the executive team stays involved in the process. There should be no surprises or major decisions taken without their being informed and having an opportunity to comment. This is a delicate balance. My experience indicates that many times, the executive team will constitute the most resistant part of the organization because of their engrained beliefs, habits and behaviors, and their reliance on past success to generate future ones.

Keeping the executive team involved helps derail sabotage and provides them with an opportunity to be part of the process. Most critical is their involvement in selecting the Innovation team and in the initial interactive SWOT analysis session.

INSIGHTS

- Carefully select a cross-organizational team comprised of operational managers at least one level below the sponsoring executive (CEO/COO).

- Team members should have experience with making data-based decisions.

- Product- and customer-facing operational personnel are critical to the success of the process; it is also helpful to have one or more business managers on the team.

- Consider relieving team members of all or part of current responsibilities to ensure adequate bandwidth and engagement in the process.

- Do not allow entrepreneurial leaders or CEO/COO direct reports to take over the process and/or quash new ideas prematurely.

Innovation Capitalizes on Internal Knowledge and External Perspective

Your organization is a valuable source of information that should not be neglected during a Pragmatic Innovation initiative. Employees live on the front lines every day and often have terrific insight into what is working—and what is not. And they often have great ideas on how to fix things.

In most of the examples included in this book, an interactive SWOT session was conducted early in the process. More on that later, but in preparation for that session, a survey of employees is invaluable. Appendix XX contains a library of questions you might consider asking.

It can also be useful to survey, or have structured discussions with, customers and partners, as well as to do some preliminary research on competitors.

For all of these endeavors, an outside resource can be extremely helpful, both in helping you sort out the most important questions to ask and in ensuring anonymity for respondents, who are more likely to provide the kind of frank and honest feedback that will help the organization if they can be assured of that anonymity.

Tapping internal knowledge is a step that is often overlooked as companies go about their strategic planning efforts, and it is a costly omission.

Insights

- Conduct a formal employee survey, either involving the entire organization, or the manager level only, to collect information relative to the effort.

- Ensure anonymity of respondents to the survey to provide a safe environment where employees can provide frank, honest responses that will confront issues existing in the organization and its culture.

- Collection of information from customers, partners and competitors is recommended prior to engaging in the first interactive SWOT session.

- Make judicious use of qualified outside resources during this initial information gathering process.

Innovation is Best When It Is Based on Data-Driven Analysis

There are a number of pragmatic strategic analyses that one should, and would, use to help drive an innovation effort. In this book, in order to maintain simplicity, I have focused on the SWOT analysis as a key element of the Pragmatic Innovation process. In a SWOT analysis, factors that affect an organization's success can generally be bucketed into four categories:

- Strengths
- Weaknesses
- Opportunities
- Threats

Thus the SWOT acronym. This is not a new concept, by any means. What is new is the Pragmatic Innovation framework in which this analysis is embedded, and the depth and intensity with which we recommend you conduct this session.

Strengths and weaknesses generally refer to internal factors, while opportunities and threats refer to factors external to the organization.

A firm's strengths are the elements and resources that provide it with a competitive advantage. These might include:

- Intellectual property
- Brand
- Good will or reputation with customers
- Technological leadership that offers price/performance benefits
- Sales channel or distribution network
- In-depth understanding of vertical or horizontal markets
- Engaged, proactive employees

Weaknesses might fall in the areas of:

- Lack of protection of intellectual property in the form of copyrights, trademarks and patents
- A base of unhappy customers who detract from the company's overall reputation
- Lack of brand recognition
- Poor price/performance
- Weak sales channel or distribution network
- Lack of market differentiation in key vertical or horizontal markets
- Unhappy employees

Sometimes a strength can also be a weakness. For example, in the printing industry, a firm with heavy investments in offset presses can consider its manufacturing capacity as an advantage. But as the market has moved more to shorter runs and on-demand production of printed product, the firm could find itself in an overcapacity situation that places a strain on finances and makes it difficult to adjust the production platform to new market requirements. At XEROX, where the investments and training had been focused on copying for so long, it was difficult to move into new areas with new technology and new business terms and conditions.

Equally important is the assessment of external factors, both in the form of opportunities and threats. Like strengths and weaknesses, opportunities and threats can also be the flip side of each other's coin. To use another printing industry example, cheap printing imported from China is a threat, but for larger printers, buying or establishing their own printing plant in China could turn this threat into an opportunity.

Examples of opportunities might include:

- Unmet customer needs
- New technology
- Favorable changes in regulations

Examples of threats might include:

- Unfavorable changes in regulations
- Alternative products entering the market
- Changes in consumer patterns, resulting in declining interest in technologies or products

Both the PC and the DocuTech were examples of capitalizing on unmet customer needs with new technologies. As IBM lost control of the PC market, it faced the threat of many alternative products with differing price/performance ratios entering the market. The same happened with Xerox and its copier dominance in the 1970s.

A SWOT analysis is an important and powerful tool that is integral to the Pragmatic Innovation process. It is not easy, however. Among other things, this type of review process may be difficult for current executives, especially when reviewing weaknesses and threats. But its purpose is to identify where a lack of focus and information exists, and it leads to the development of a meaningful action plan.

For these reasons, it is often helpful to invite an outside facilitator—or a professional facilitator from inside the company, if you have one—to conduct the session. Good facilitation and the open influence of the CEO/COO can turn this session into an invaluable source of needed information about customer requirements, the competition, and required internal process improvements that will lead the way to an innovative future.

Depending on how insulated from the outside world the organization has been in terms of recent new staff additions at the executive and management level, it may be necessary to augment the team with new members from outside the organization. This worked effectively at Xerox and Gulfstream, as I have related.

It is my experience that if the team members have been in countless meetings together over the years, and there is minimal "new blood" as you embark on your Pragmatic Innovation journey, the answers and approach will be too insular, much less effective, and the old paradigm of the organization will strangle the success of the effort. It is like many companies today that locate employees virtually and expect them to work together on the strength of shared e-mails.

At the conclusion of the interactive SWOT session, you should have a list of internal and external data gathering needs to fill identified gaps in knowledge, as well as a very preliminary list of potential opportunities for the innovation team to explore.

The innovation team should develop a straw man set of project objectives at this time and be segmented into data gathering teams to verify the expectations and probable conclusions developed in the first interactive SWOT. A definitive schedule should be established for data gathering and alternative action evaluations. Outside resources can also be engaged for data gathering and alternative action evaluations. Outside resources will augment the team to make data gathering from competitors and partners more effective.

Without a definitive schedule and action items with clear accountability attached, the effort can easily become bogged down at this point. However, in my experience, these sessions create a high level of enthusiasm and excitement about the future of the company. That enthusiasm and excitement goes a long way toward carrying the momentum in these early stages. Capitalize on it with frequent communication between the team leader and the team, including frequent status and information-sharing meetings to keep the momentum going.

INSIGHTS

- During the planning process for the session, educate the team on the SWOT process so they can gain an understanding of the process and begin thinking about the strengths, weaknesses, opportunities and threats the company is facing.

- Develop a list of questions to be asked of stakeholders—including employees, partners and customers—prior to the session, and assign someone to seek out competitive information that is perceived to be useful in the overall effort.

- Conduct pre-session research, including surveys, and compile results for presentation at the meeting.

- If you are planning to augment staff to introduce new blood to the innovation team, that should be done prior to this first interactive SWOT session to gain maximum value from the session, and from the insight new team members can bring.

- Prior to the session, compile survey results and prepare to present them to the group overall as a basis for discussion.

- Conduct a facilitated off-site meeting focused on creating an in-depth SWOT analysis involving all stakeholders.

- Plan to exit the meeting with information gaps identified and a preliminary list of opportunities.

- Consider engaging a professional facilitator who is experienced in conducting these types of sessions.

- By engaging all leaders across your organization with information, there is more likely to be early buy-in on the part of both the core and extended innovation teams.

- Assign team members specific data gathering tasks with a definitive timeline attached.

- Conduct frequent update and status sessions to maintain momentum and ensure that team members are tracking to the timeline.

- Consider engaging outside resources to acquire information from competitors/partners.

- Compile findings into a presentation and/or report for use by the team as work proceeds.

Innovation Can Benefit from Benchmarking

It will be very important during this period to develop information with enough quality to allow benchmarking of processes, products, services and customer satisfaction against competitors and other similar companies in the industry. It is not unusual for big opportunities for improvement to be revealed during this process. An example, as noted in this book, was the need to utilize color and custom forms to support new VSBs at NEBS.

I have never seen this process fail to produce important new information, such as the need to change IBM's terms and conditions to be successful as a personal computer vendor, or the need for the Xerox DocuTech to offer connectivity. It can also act to unhook strategies which might not deliver success in the marketplace, based on research. That was the case with the supersonic jet at Gulfstream.

INSIGHTS

- Use data collected and analyses generated as a result of the SWOT to benchmark processes, products, services and customer satisfaction against competitors.

- Conduct additional research to validate "big ideas" that come out of work to date; i.e., similar to the research we conducted to validate the needs of VSBs at NEBS.

- Take necessary steps to terminate projects which might be underway that are demonstrated by this effort to lack the appropriate level of market viability, such as we did with the supersonic business jet project at Gulfstream.

Innovation Recommendations Should Be Prioritized and Consensus-Based

Once data is gathered and the innovation team has become comfortable with prioritizing potential new directions, it is time to conduct the next joint Executive Team and Innovation Team meeting, led by the overall leader (i.e., the CEO/COO). In my experience, this would take place three to six months after starting the overall process. Of course, this work has been going on in parallel with the normal process of running the business, so the use of outside facilities for this meeting is helpful. Care must be taken to keep the innovation team involved and owning the results of the process. That is the role Frank

Carey played as we presented to the Corporate Management Committee at IBM, and it was invaluable to the overall success of the program.

A decision must be made at this time regarding which, if any, of the new opportunities identified should be staffed and pursued. Based on those decisions, leaders are assigned responsibility for the implementation of new initiatives, and assigned resources must be applied against specific schedules, achievement expectations or benchmarks.

In the IBM case, this was represented by my assignment with responsibility for the development of the PC with the approval of resources against a schedule expectation. At Xerox, this was the assignment to develop a connectivity strategy and an industry connectivity plan for the DocuTech. At NEBS, it was the decision to create a custom/color product line with appropriate changes in the marketing catalog, and manufacturing and distribution plans.

I remember another talk with Frank Carey where he impressed upon a group of us the appropriate way to have an organization take on new work. He said, "You begin with strategy, then you set up the structure you need to succeed. Then you carefully proceed with appropriate staffing." My friend Joe Trapodi, who recently took over the marketing reigns at Coca Cola, tells me that is exactly how he is approaching his new assignment there.

It is important to ensure clear communication of new directions to the operational teams that will carry out these initiatives. It is also important to clearly communicate the intention to proceed with various opportunities to segments of the organization who may be threatened by this new direction.

It is natural for segments of a large organization to be threatened by change. That is why Frank Carey's conditions were put in place regarding IBM's non-concurrence process, to ensure that the organization did not overwhelm the PC team.

Effective internal communications should act to allay those fears for the most part. When they cannot be allayed, obstructionist actions must be prevented from derailing the process.

Insights

- Convene a joint Executive/Implementation Team meeting to review results of the work to date.

- Expected outcome plays into the decision about which, if any, of the identified opportunities should be staffed and pursued.

- Leaders and resources must be freed up at this time to pursue opportunities of interest.

- It is critical to keep the innovation team involved and owning the results of the process.

- Develop and deploy effective internal communications to ensure that all constituencies are notified about and engaged in the process as appropriate.

- This step requires clear leadership from the CEO/COO and should offer a way for the innovation team to work around obstructionist activities—should they occur—with the least amount of disruption to the overall process.

Innovation Feeds on Continuous Improvement

Once a new direction is established, ensure that your implementation plan includes benchmarks for achievement and periodic measurements on progress. Many organizations use Six Sigma or other extensive quality tools.

These can be valuable as long as people do not cripple the team with extreme over-management, delaying the forward momentum of the Pragmatic Innovation process. At Xerox, for example, its mature Leadership Through Quality process could often add extensive time and bureaucracy to any activity, unless closely managed.

Also, ensure that your new plan addresses the marketing, promotion, and business terms and conditions required for success.

Many companies make the mistake of forcing new ideas, products, services and strategic directions into their established processes and cultures. Do not make the mistake that Xerox made with many inventions that came out of PARC, including the personal computer. Consider bringing in outside help to challenge your organization's traditional way of doing things.

Innovation activities often cause particular concern in legal and financial organizations. The innovation team leader must push to gain acceptance of the terms and conditions required to make a new offering successful. This was quite a battle at IBM and went against the grain of long-established principles. But in the end, with the support of Frank Carey, we were able to do what we needed to do to get the job done.

For a large organization, getting this right will be one of the most significant challenges because of a tendency to support uniformity and consistency around the old platform as I experienced at IBM and other companies.

At a minimum, companies must establish plans to manage new projects against quantitative goals. In order to continue an innovation mindset beyond this initial project, a company can schedule periodic updates, including revisiting the SWOT process, to gauge progress and ensure continued generation of fresh ideas. It is possible to put someone in place to manage innovation, but that would require formal procedures to make sure that the process did not stagnate in the engrained culture. If such a position is desired, perhaps rotating personnel through that role every few years will help keep things fresh.

An innovative company is dependent on its leader to provide the direction, protection and continuous focus on new ideas. The person I admire most, who provides this kind of leadership today, is Steve Jobs. I know he continually sponsors innovation within Apple; develops a spirit of change to derail old, existing paradigms; and surrounds himself with people who are always stretching the envelope—and he encourages them to do so.

Other companies who have done a good job of fostering innovation include General Electric, Rolls Royce, Caterpillar and EMC, all with different but effective strategies.

INSIGHTS

- Establish benchmarks for achievement and periodic measurements on progress.

- Take care not to let organizational inertia overcome the proliferation of innovation beyond the first project.

- If you choose to put an "Innovation Czar" in place, rotate that position frequently to keep it fresh.

- Manage new projects against quantitative goals.

- Schedule periodic updates, including revisiting the SWOT process, to gauge progress and ensure continuing generation of fresh ideas.

- As the leader of the organization, take care to foster innovation and drive ongoing change in the organization.

CHAPTER 9

Taking No-Nonsense Innovation into the Public Sector

"I felt that I could make a difference.
That's the best reason to go into business."

SIR RICHARD BRANSON (1950 -)

BRITISH ENTREPRENEUR, CHAIRMAN OF VIRGIN GROUP

W ith our latest project, it seems like things have come full circle. Open Innovation has worked with new hardware and systems products like the IBM PC, the DocuTech and the Gulfstream V. The process we have developed supported the growth in customer services at New England Business Services and in a software-based service business at Proamics. At NEPS, our newly developed strategy is helping us blend software and a customer communications management service model in a fast growing industry. In an increasingly global economy, innovation occurring in one part of the world can easily and quickly have an effect—positive or negative—on other parts of the world.

Don Tapscott, in his recent best seller, *Wikinomics*[1], says, "In China, 'innovation cities' are emerging across the country where thousands of intermingling companies leverage technology, low-cost structures and physical proximity to destroy their worldwide competition. The world provides a diverse set of environments for innovation, depending on factors like technology infrastructure, country-specific skills, income levels and competitive dynamics." I would add that when considering innovation, one of the greatest assets any country has is the focus and commitment it places on the quality of education for its students.

Until now, this has been a tremendous area of frustration for me, especially in the American education system. When Ted Nelson said we were going to bring "all information to everyone, when and where they wanted it no matter where they were," it appeared to be a vision that was viable everywhere exception education. Now we are trying to do something about that situation.

---

1   *Wikinomics: How Mass Collaboration Changes Everything,* Expanded Edition, by Don Tapscott and Anthony D. Williams, The Penguin Group, 2008

An Educational Crisis

Remember the story of Rip Van Winkle? Asleep for 100 years, he awoke to a very strange world. Yet a common anecdote that surfaces in education circles is that Rip Van Winkle would not recognize the world of business, and would surely be impressed with how technology has changed what a typical corporate or manufacturing facility looks like and how it operates compared to 100 years ago. He would be amazed at how technology has driven efficiencies and improved healthcare in hospitals. He would even applaud how government uses technology, with NASA as one example, and the Government Printing Office implementation of FD-SYS, as another, with its futuristic information management system that ensures protection of government documents, data and information in perpetuity. Yet when Rip Van Winkle walks into a classroom after napping for 20 years, he would instantly recognize the institution. Just about the only thing that has changed is the blackboard, which is now white instead of green. In many schools, the textbooks are old, antiquated and no longer as relevant as the information that can be accessed instantly on the Internet. Rip Van Winkle would also be impressed with how much information is now available to students in an open content environment but perhaps saddened by the inability for the education system to effectively incorporate this vast knowledge source into the curriculum.

Wikipedia founder Jimmy Wales states it well when he says, "Imagine a world in which every single person on the planet is given free access to the sum of all human knowledge. That's what we're doing." And that is what this final chapter is all about for me.

As I have explained earlier, the move IBM made to an open content approach with the launch of the PC represented perhaps the most revolutionary thinking and transformation one could have undertaken at the time at Big Blue. And though at times the company has retrenched from a cooperative versus a proprietary approach in its market stance, today IBM has re-emerged as a corporate technology leader, years ahead of many of its competitors, working positively with new partners and open source communities to build a positive and innovative business model.

As Tapscott and Williams said in *Wikonomics*, "IBM was an unlikely candidate to become a champion of peer production and leader of the open world. After all, we're talking about Big Blue—the company that became huge by building and selling proprietary everything. For decades it created software that only worked on IBM computers. Tough luck if you wanted to port it to another vendor's hardware. IBM called it 'account control.' Detractors called it 'hotel proprietary.' That is, you can check out any time you like, but you can never leave. In a stunning reversal of strategy (and fortune), IBM has embraced open source at the core of its business in a way few organizations of its size and maturity have dared." I believe this was largely due to the leadership of Frank Carey back in the 1970s and 1980s and his willingness to accept the revolutionary proposal we submitted to him more than twenty-five years ago which set a positive experiential base for the company and proved that open innovative practices could deliver positive business results.

It is all coming full circle now for me. I am currently involved in a project that merges innovation in both technology and open content sourcing, and I am working with IBM in this venture, engaging in a global green effort that involves recycling and refurbishing PCs to improve the educational experience for students, particularly in math and science. This is the most exciting innovation project I have undertaken in a long time. We are developing a truly new education open source ecosystem that has started to bloom. Let me explain.

Cristina and I have worked with a number of technology companies over the years that have attempted to deliver the promise of the information age and the power of modern computing technology to primary and secondary schools. One such company in Arizona tried to deliver a one-to-one (1:1) educational instruction software program to a number of school environments without much success. Through this effort, though, we began to share our commitment to educational innovation by working with representatives of the Gates Foundation for Education.

In fairness to the educational community, there have been a number of major obstacles to the progress of 1:1 education. Fully loaded PCs are too expensive to maintain, and their total cost of ownership is prohibitive for most district budgets to be able to afford a PC for each child. In addition, there are ongoing reliability issues and the traditional Microsoft interface presents many complex situations that demand added IT resources, which many school districts can ill afford. Power and cooling requirements for server-based models must also be taken into consideration, especially with the skyrocketing costs of energy. Even inexpensive laptops require ongoing upgrades to software and expensive software licensing fees increasing the total cost of ownership for this computing equipment, and creating severe budgetary barriers to adoption, especially within major inner city school districts.

Teachers want to teach. Managing technology is not their number one priority, nor should it be. Thus it is rare that you find teachers who want to embrace software technologies in their classroom given all of the other demands placed upon them for performance and compliance with State regulations and requirements.

Some wealthy communities and well endowed private educational institutions have the resources to support the addition of upgraded laptops, the latest software and enriching and motivational content to their curriculum, but these schools remain in the minority. On the opposite end of the spectrum, there are large inner city schools that can't even graduate 50 percent of their high school students, and few of those who do graduate go on to college or university. Clearly, technology has not impacted these students in any positive way, and yet they need to be skilled in basic core subjects, they need to interact with computers and technology as they enter the work force, and having an understanding of the role of technology is the only way their future can be ensured in an increasingly competitive world.

John Chambers, Chairman and CEO of Cisco Systems, once said, "The next big killer application for the Internet is going to be education. Education over the Internet (virtual) is going to be so big, it is going to make e-mail usage look like a rounding error."

Cristina and I heartily agree with Chambers. As a result, we are now involved in a new company, QWK2LRN that is positioned to make a difference in finally delivering to our primary and secondary educational institutions the promise envisioned by Ted Nelson. But none of this could even have gotten started without our first major client understanding and embracing Pragmatic Innovation. We had to be on the same page in that regard in order to make the kind of progress needed for mutual success because while this is a public sector endeavor, it requires true out-of-the-box thinking on the part of all participants, and it also requires a fact-based approach that can break through the barriers of both "business as usual" and the extreme financial constraints many of our educational institutions face today.

Our children, Danny and Gabriela, who are text messaging aficionados,
selected the name of our new venture.

This book is about the Pragmatic Innovation process. In it, we have learned that the first step is to identify a leadership team and ensure full support of the executive team; both must signal a readiness to tackle issues with new thinking. For those participating in the process, there is a need for consensus that innovative change is crucial in order to propel the organization into a new future. A painful but honest assessment of internal strengths and weaknesses must be undertaken using valid and reliable data points. At the same time, there is a need for the team to conduct an external benchmarking effort to understand the roles and emerging needs of customers, suppliers and business partners with a goal of discovering potential new paths of engagement. The management team and the innovation team, whether in a business or educational environment, must both demonstrate a willingness to accept outside ideas and recommendations, and must work hard to grasp alternative approaches rather than relying on the practices and processes that have made them successful in the past. There is also a need to periodically refresh organizational thinking to ensure that the overall process is working and that new ideas continue to emerge and be taken advantage of appropriately.

Pragmatic Innovation is not a theoretical exercise. As discussed in this book, we have utilized this model to create dramatic success in as little as 90 days. We are very excited about its potential to create yet another successful venture in the field of education. While it is rewarding to reinvent a business, reinventing our educational system will have much more far-reaching effects than any single business could ever achieve.

It is quite fitting that this new venture is being developed in partnership with IBM, another example of the world coming full circle. I left IBM 20 years ago. Since that time, the mix of business at IBM has changed, but the character of the company and its "can do" attitude has not. After working on a variety of projects and interacting with numerous large companies during the past 20 years, it has been refreshing working with IBM on this project over the past few months. There is no question that IBM has had its issues over the years, but this recent experience has reinforced for me just how fortunate I was to begin my career with Big Blue. Even though I am not an employee, I have to say that it feels great to be back in a relationship with a company of the quality of IBM.

It is also rewarding to see that dormant and unused PCs can be resurrected and given a second life that will transform the lives of many young people globally. We must stop dumping "obsolete" computers in our landfills and waste sites, and our current venture offers a way to mitigate that activity.

IBM remains extremely generous in its corporate giving and heartfelt commitment. We are fortunate also to have the support of several major foundations and companies. Together, we will pragmatically innovate in education, and we believe we will make a difference. Let's let Rip Van Winkle nap for a few more short years. When he awakes, we believe he will see a very different education landscape.

QWK2LRN

So what is this venture all about and how does it leverage Pragmatic Innovation?

This project carries the moniker of QWK2LRN. It began with two ex-IBM technical experts, Jim Hare and Chuck Hale, who wanted to make a difference by delivering technology-based education to underprivileged, under resourced urban educational environments. Their first priority was their home town of Detroit, where currently only 25 percent of high school students complete high school[2]. This devastating state of affairs is replicated

---

2   The Detroit public school graduation rate is 24.9 percent. Source: Education Week's Diploma County: Ready for What? Nationwide, 1.23 million high school seniors will not graduate in 2008 (Source: Education Week)

across the country at varying levels and means that more than one million students who start ninth grade in the United States fail to get their high school diploma. The problem is magnified in Detroit, a community that has both the highest poverty rate[3] and the highest unemployment rate[4] in the United States. Hare and Hale believed if they could be a positive agent of change in Detroit, their model could be successful anywhere.

The initial thrust of the technology was to take the components most likely to fail out of personal computers, replace the Microsoft interface with a web-based Google or Yahoo! interface and test these refurbished machines inside a few selected public and private schools with the help of the technology incubator program from Wayne State University. Hare and Hale took this program through four years of rigorous development and day-to-day operational improvements. As they prepared to launch the project to a wider audience, Cristina and I were introduced to them by Jonathan Webb, Managing Partner of Green Pastures Partners[5], and we became engaged in the project as consultants to leverage the principles of Pragmatic Innovation as the project was taken to its next phase. While these two innovators had done an outstanding job thus far of developing this breakthrough solution to our educational woes, their next step would require interaction with mainstream educational institutions and, like many attempts in the past, without leveraging

---

3 Detroit has the highest poverty rate among the 20 largest American cities, and the Detroit median household income of $28,069 is the lowest among these cities, according to the U.S. Census Bureau.

4 Michigan's jobless rate in May 2008 was 6.9 percent, the highest in the nation. Michigan lost 28,700 jobs in the period March through May 2008, according to a Bureau of Labor statistical analysis performed by MBG Information Services.

5 Jonathan Hudson Webb is the Managing Partner of Green Pastures Partners (GPP), a Chicago-based independent private equity firm. As a member of the Investment Committee, Mr. Webb oversees buyout and growth investments of $5 - $40 million in equity capital; and he also serves on the boards of the firm's portfolio companies.

Pragmatic Innovation, they would be unlikely to achieve success due to the resistance they would undoubtedly face with a conventional approach.

As I write this, we are preparing to architect and present a comprehensive thin client solution for 1:1 computing utilizing the Pragmatic Innovation model. We are working with the new Superintendent of Detroit Public Schools and her new team of innovators. Ms. Lafayette as the operations leader for the Superintendent is an ideal leader candidate because she has a strong technology background and good strategic vision. Ms. Appling, a tenured principal, has been designated to lead the innovation program into the District's 20 high schools. As part of the preparation, we performed a great deal of benchmarking with successful 1:1 initiatives, and reviewed various technology offerings, software and content information. All of this material has been discussed and shared, along with many white papers and other academic material on this emerging trend in education. This preparation was the basis for an in-depth SWOT analysis.

The SWOT analysis revealed that to scale, launch and achieve top tier performance with the QWK2LRN technology model, IBM would be an ideal partner. Many of the weaknesses the District needs to overcome are driven by its poor reputation among many partners, vendors, suppliers and parent groups. Yet, this analysis, though painful for the District, served to fuel the notion that a major shift had to occur and a technology initiative with proper discipline and strategic vision was essential at this critical juncture for the District.

As for the QWK2LRN initiative itself, the group has embraced many innovative changes in a short period of time. The organization has new executive management, a new model for sales and marketing, a new brand and image, a positive IBM partnership in place, a set of supportive suppliers, a global vision, and most importantly, an ingrained belief that innovation is not only essential for the successful development and ongoing deployment of the technology, but in the business processes of the organization as well. There are plans to roll this concept out to other cities in North and South America, and the timing will be based, in part, on the results we achieve in Detroit.

I am pleased to remain in support of this exciting new initiative as the non-Executive Chairman helping to steer much of the direction in what I believe is the final frontier for PC technology in education, a legacy I am proud of.

Appendix D includes information about the QWK2LRN initiative for readers that may wish to get involved as we work to improve worldwide education.

Take Charge

Innovation drives new products and services. It is a key to improving our way of life. I hope this book will lead to new ideas, initiatives, and changes that will improve your business and deliver the full benefits of Pragmatic Innovation to you and your organization.

Please also join us at www.PragmaticInnovation.net, where we are establishing an active community of like-minded business innovators who wish to dialog and share Pragmatic Innovation experiences. We will also be building a library of tips and tools over time to broaden the Pragmatic Innovation experience. We hope this community will have an impact on the business and educational landscape in North America as well as in other parts of the world, generating a wealth of ideas that can be deployed for the greater good. We look forward to seeing you there!

APPENDIX A

Sample SWOT Questions

I n mid-2007, Cristina and I facilitated an interactive SWOT session at NEPS, where I was CEO. A substantial amount of time was invested in developing pre-session surveys, collecting and analyzing responses to make the interactive SWOT more productive. These questions are shared in this Appendix with the hope that they will help you speed up the process of constructing your own pre-session surveys.

This session was conducted shortly after the acquisition of APT, and was all the more valuable for being able to include representation from both organizations.

The Company

1. What is your current vision for the company?
2. How would you describe the company in one sentence?

3. What is our current mission statement?

4. Where do you see the company by this time next year?

5. In five years?

6. How would you describe the culture of the company?

7. Can you list the core values by which you would like to operate the business?

8. What personality do you associate with the company?

9. What are your desired perceptions of the company? That is, how do you want your customers, strategic partners and the overall marketplace to think of us?

Marketing

10. What do you feel is your most difficult marketing challenge?

11. What aspects of your marketing strategy need the most focus or attention?

12. How well do you feel the current company name represents your business?

13. What is the company's international plan?

Market Conditions

14. Are there any legislative requirements, technical advances or trends that could change the course of your business?

Acquisition

15. If acquisition is part of the company strategy, what types of companies would you most likely be interested in?

16. What types of companies do you think would bring the most value and why?

Products/Services

17. What is your near-term product/service development strategy and timeline?

18. What is your long-range product/service strategy?

19. What positive feelings are associated with our products/services?

20. What negative feelings are associated with our products/services?

21. What are your desired perceptions for our products/services?

22. Are there any associations we should be careful to avoid?

Sales and Distribution

23. What are your primary channels/methods for acquiring your customers?

24. What are your secondary channels/methods for acquiring your customers?

25. What is the typical sales process from the initial contact to close?

26. Who is the primary target audience for each product/service?

27. Who is the secondary target audience for each product/service?

28. What business problems are these target audiences in need of solving?

29. Who needs to be influenced in the purchase decision? Titles? Who actually makes the purchase decision?

30. What other audiences are important?

31. What benefits and results can the end user (our customer's customer) expect from us?
    What benefits and results can our customer expect from us?

32. Why should the user trust us?
    Why should the customer trust us?

33. What are the most important messages to communicate to the end user?

    What are the most important messages to communicate to the customer?

Competition

34. Who are the competitors in your primary target audience?

    Who are the competitors in your secondary target audience?

35. What is the primary difference between you and the competition?

36. What is your distinctive advantage over your competition?

    What is your primary disadvantage over your competition?

APPENDIX B

Executive/Innovation Team Workshop

After the SWOT

This appendix provides a suggested guideline for the joint Executive/ Innovation Team session that is conducted following the interactive SWOT analysis and the innovation team's subsequent work.

STRATEGIC PLANS

"A good deal of corporate planning … is like a ritual rain dance. It has no effect on the weather that follows … Much of the advice related to corporate planning is directed at improving the dancing, not the weather"

JAMES BRIAN QUINN

Pragmatic Innovation is directed at improving the weather. The desired outcome of this workshop is a balanced perspective between issues and opportunities.

The outline contained in this appendix is an example only. It is a compilation from actual sessions conducted with various companies with whom I have worked and does not represent one company. It is a framework that I have found to be effective and can easily be modified for use with any organization.

Agenda

- Executive Summary
- Team Assumptions
- The Mission Statement
- Market Sizing
- Technology Update
- Financials: Outlook and Gap
- Issues Going Forward
- Opportunities
- Recommendations

Executive Summary

This portion of the agenda kicks the meeting off and sets the stage for the rest of the session.

- Reaffirm direction of the last plan
    - o   List major business areas here

- Identify critical issues
    - o   List of critical issues (examples included here)
    - o   Cost structure
    - o   Expansion
    - o   New product offering

- o Product development process
- o Information technology infrastructure
- o Organizational competencies
- o Profitability

- • Recommend additional opportunities
  - o Several to focus on
  - o Many to experiment with

- • In a nutshell, we must …
  - o Get our costs in line
  - o Put some resources behind a few new initiatives
  - o Germinate another 10 initiatives

Team Assumptions

- • Team Charter
  - o Review current strategic business plan
  - o Confirm market size and target market numbers
  - o Identify operational issues associated with the successful execution of the plan
  - o Describe and size additional business opportunities
  - o Incorporate plans for all business units

- • Operating Principle
  - o Leadership is the act of productively maintaining tension between where you want to be (Vision) and where you are (Reality). We kept this in mind throughout our efforts.

The Mission Statement

In the case of NEBS, the team suggested a new mission statement that more accurately reflected its business. It was simple, easy to understand, and limited the target customer while broadening the possibilities. It presented a customer-in versus a Product-Out view.

"We are the Small Business Resource."

Market Sizing

- Discuss areas of growth and decline
- Quick take at competitive landscape, including share and penetration for each segment
- Does current market sizing data support strategic plan?

Technology Update

- What has changed, and what has not, in the technology infrastructure?

- Where are perceived gaps and what might their impact be?

Financials: Outlook and Gap

ISSUES GOING FORWARD

- The market for the base business is mature and declining, and it is the funding source for our future

- Many of the competencies required for our future (technology, channel, product) are markedly different than we have today

- Key issues that must be addressed in order to meet financial outlook:
  - o Cost structure
  - o Channel expansion
  - o New products
  - o Product development process
  - o Information technology infrastructure
  - o Organizational competencies

- Develop a specific action or set of actions to address each issue. This should include accountability for accomplishing the action or managing its accomplishment.

Opportunities

- Based on preceding work and discussions, the innovation team presents recommended opportunities that have been developed prior to the session, as a direct result of the previous interactive SWOT analysis.
- Recommendations are supported with data gathered during the post-SWOT phase

Recommendations

- The combined Executive/Innovative Team should leave this session with a prioritized list of recommended projects.

- Following the session, the innovation team will collect additional data and begin work on recommended opportunities

- At this stage, frequent communication between the executive team and the innovation team is essential.

APPENDIX C

Vision and Mission, A Primer

Vision/Mission

Vision without action is merely a dream. Action without vision just passes the time. Vision with action can change the world.

JOEL BARKER

Background

A vision and mission statement are a two-part description of overall business intent. The Vision Statement describes the future, where you are going or where you want to go. The Mission Statement describes today: why you exist today and what you are doing to pursue your vision of the future. Together they provide direction for the business by focusing attention on doing things day-to-day to accomplish your mission, while taking steps to pursue your vision of the future – your long-term business intent.

A solid vision, documented as the Vision Statement, creates commitment and understanding. It enables your team to focus on the future, and it enables others to understand how the top of the organization visualizes the future. Initially, it is a dream that with the right plan, personnel, commitment and execution can come to fruition. The statement must not be bland and boring, but should be heartfelt enough to excite and inspire those who read it to take action. The words should also reflect the values the organization actually lives by rather than those it believes it ought to live by.

Mission Statements are intended to focus attention on essentials, and to summarize the essential core competencies and/or capabilities of the business. They also help to concentrate the efforts of the management team and employees on desired focal points.

The Mission Statement should:

* be narrow enough to give direction and guidance to everyone in the business;

* be large enough to allow the business to grow and realize its potential;

* be realistic, achievable and brief; and

* capture the essence of an organization without being so vague it could apply to any organization.

Examples:

Xerox

. . . give customers better ways to do great work.

. . . offering a coherent and architected set of document solutions and services, enabling new business opportunities and enhancing the value of Xerox devices.

Federal Express

"FedEx is committed to our People-Service-Profit Philosophy. We will produce outstanding financial returns by providing totally reliable, competitively superior, global, air-ground transportation of high-priority goods and documents that require rapid, time-certain delivery."

Saturn

"Our mission is to earn the loyalty of Saturn owners and grow our family by developing and marketing U.S.-manufactured vehicles that are world leaders in quality, cost, and customer enthusiasm through the integration of people, technology, and business systems."

Westin Hotels and Resorts

Mission:

"In order to realize our Vision, our Mission must be to exceed the expectations of our customers, whom we define as guests, partners, and fellow employees.

We will accomplish this by committing to our shared values and by achieving the highest levels of customer satisfaction, with extraordinary emphasis on the creation of value. In this way we will ensure that our profit, quality and growth goals are met."

Vision:

"Year after year, Westin and its people will be regarded as the best and most sought after hotel and resort management group in North America."

APPENDIX D

QWK2LRN

A Systematic Approach

As we have seen in other Pragmatic Innovation examples throughout this book, successful innovation initiatives require a systematic approach. From the perspective of a school district wishing to evolve to a 1:1 computing model, a systematic approach is likely to require:

- Building public and political support for needed change

- Building professional support within the District and the local business community for needed change

- Providing adequate financial support and resources

- Determining through analysis an appropriate technical architecture

- Building proper partnerships and establishing collaborators to sustain change

- Establishing realistic objectives for initial and long term implementation

- Assigning and empowering persons responsible for goal achievement

- Establishing an administrative culture of support for fundamental changes from traditional practices

- Supporting teacher and student initiatives to create student-centered, constructivist classrooms

Districts must establish a set of 1:1 goals, which might include:

- Improve equity of access to technology
- Improve the quality of learning
- Improve attendance in core subjects
- Improve student learning and retention of content
- Increase performance on standardized testing
- Improve student ability to become lifelong learners
- Prepare students for the world of work
- Improve home-school connection

This requires a frank and honest assessment of the current state on the part of all stakeholders, especially the teachers. Teachers and administrators should take a hard look at how they have integrated technology into the core curriculum. Where do they rate along an assessment rubric continuum?

- **Level I:** I have my students go to computer lab where teacher supervises them. I have not incorporated technology as part of my curriculum.

- **Level II**: I have programs on a few computers in the classroom but used as a stand-alone program and as a supplement to the curriculum. Usually working on a project that the computer teacher developed.

- **Level III:** I use my computer to present projects and sometimes my students use technology for writing projects.

- **Level IV:** I have reviewed the curriculum and found technology resources that enhance student learning.

- **Level V**: I am interested in creating exciting curriculum that motivates students, and I have invented new strategies of using technology as part of the curriculum. I benchmark what other teachers in the same grade and subject are doing with technology as part of the curriculum.

- **Level VI:** My students create exciting projects that expand the curriculum. I collaborate with other teachers so we are not reinventing the wheel. I have partnerships with companies, parents and others to seek new ways of teaching and learning.

The 1:1 Computing Challenge: Implementation and Sustainability

As mentioned earlier, the cost of computers is a major challenge to financially constrained school districts. Traditional 1:1 laptop computing models are expensive to initiate, with a cost of $800 to $1,500 per laptop. And the costs go beyond simply acquiring computers and software. It is costly to maintain the integrity of the devices. They are fragile and prone to breakage and theft. Ongoing technical support can be expensive, as much as $1,000 to $1,500 per unit per year. Add to that the cost of maintaining the integrity of the network and the operating system and other software on each machine, and the situation becomes even more expensive and complex, requiring highly skilled IT people on staff, a luxury many school districts simply cannot afford.

As districts develop their 1:1 computing programs, they must plan for the technological infrastructure required to support the initiative. This includes computers, software, wired and wireless networks, services and other things required in the data center. The infrastructure investment generally consumes the largest portion of a project budget, though it can be as little as 20 percent of the overall total cost of ownership for the entire deployed system, including classroom computers.

QWK2LRN's Innovative 1:1 Computing Solution

At QWK2LRN, based on the work of Hare and Hale, we have developed a unique and revolutionary technology that offers greater reliability, capability, speed, safety, scalability and flexibility than any previous laptop or 1:1 computing model that has been introduced to the marketplace. In the classroom, it requires an Internet connection and electricity, so beyond the infrastructure investment the District must make, it is extremely affordable.

QWK2LRN uses a thin client model that is easily maintained and requires little technical on-site support. Thin client, sometimes also called lean client, is a computer that depends primarily on a central server for processing activities and is primarily focused on conveying input and output between the user and the remote server. In contrast, a thick or fat client does as much processing as possible and passes only data for communications and storage to the server.[1] With limited processing requirements at the client, or individual computer workstation, a much less expensive configuration can be utilized.

This model delivers a sustainable solution with a technology lifespan of seven to ten years—a much longer lifespan than previously achievable. It also means that less functional computing hardware is required in the classroom, and computers discarded by businesses and others as obsolete can be recycled to create these thin client workstations. This has the benefit of reducing costs and helping the environment by reducing the amount of obsolete computer equipment that ends up in the landfill.

The thin client model also means that there is no need for a hard disk at the individual workstation. This increases reliability and significant reduces electricity consumption, another cost and environmental benefit of the program. In fact, these thin client computers consume at least one-third less power than conventional computers.

In the QWK2LRN model, there is an Internet Scale Computing Facility (ISCF) that is located off-site. This means that the schools do not need to invest in the servers or the specialized facilities for a server farm. Student workstations are connected via the Internet to the ISCF, which can support thousands of student workstations. The thin client workstation appears to the student as a full-function PC but does not need an individual PC operating system or application software. QWK2LRN supports all Internet browsers and standards, and has a unique architecture that scales in 11 dimensions providing linear scalability to support any workload. This architecture means that there are no critical load points such as simultaneous database access that might cause performance slowdowns or failures in a conventional client/server model.

---

1 Source: Wikipedia, April 15, 2008

This also means that the school district has limited infrastructure needs, and much of the content, at least in early projects, is being donated by foundations and companies in collaboration with QWK2LRN. Among other things, ventilated, raised floor server rooms are not required for this project.

As a further cost reduction, QWK2LRN uses Open Source software applications and courseware, and its architecture both reduces technical support requirements drastically and protects school districts from piracy lawsuits and the effects of malware or questionable software vendor practices.

Our initial analysis sows a three-year savings over conventional projects of nearly $750,000 for a 300-seat deployment, as shown in the figures below.

Cost Comparison (300 seats)

Traditional 1:1 Laptop Initiative

v. QWK2LRN Model

	Traditional Laptop Initiative	QWK2LRN	QWK2LRN Savings
Installation	$1,000 per laptop x 300 seats (only cost of device) Total Cost: **$300,000**	$500 per seat (devices, furniture, installation, wiring, etc.) 300 seats = $150,000 Total cost: **$150,000**	Save **$150,000** Initially
Maintenance and Technical Support	Industry average - $750 per seat x 300 seats Total Cost = **$225,000**	$100 per seat x 300 seats Total Cost **$30,000**	Save **$195,000** yearly
Replacement costs	Calculated at 5% a year 15 seats x $1,000 each Total Cost = **$15,000**	Included in per seat subscription/technical annual support fee. Total cost = $0	Save **$15,000** yearly

QWK2LRN.com

THREE-YEAR COST COMPARISON, 300 SEATS

	Laptop Initiative	QWK2LRN	Three year savings QWK2LRN Model
Year 1 – Installation	$300,000	$150,000	$345,000
Year 1 – Maintenance/Technical Support	$225,000	$30,000	
Year 2 Yearly fee/replacement costs	$225,000	$30,000	$195,000
Year 3 Yearly fee/replacement costs	$225,000	$30,000	$195,000
TOTAL – 3 year cost	**$975,000**	**$240,000**	**$735,000**

It has the added benefit of being "Green." The system uses refurbished, existing PC inventories already available at schools and/or learning centers or donated by organizations who would otherwise simply discard them. This reclaims life for old and discarded systems and prevents unnecessary additions to landfill. As part of our project, QWK2LRN is contracting with suppliers to provide these refurbished PCs and laptops. As indicated, the QWK2LRN model typically uses one-third of the power, and power consumption for services is consolidated in the shared ISCF facility.

Finally, the ISCF shared model means that QWK2LRN can be deployed virtually anywhere in the world. So while we have focused our discussion so far on North America, and specifically our pilot project in Detroit, this model can be rolled out globally, including underserved developing countries, and has the potential of revolutionizing education worldwide. Users need only provide appropriate electrical outlets and an internet connection. We have even been able to successful deploy this using dial-up! In exchange for a modest annual maintenance and support fee, schools have the assurance that in the event of theft, equipment failure, breakage, etc., the units will be replaced at no extra charge, and generally within five days, to ensure continuity of use.

This is a unique and revolutionary model for the future. We expect it to:

- Increase student achievement.

- Transform instruction, making it more relevant and engaging (thus reducing dropout rates).

- Differentiate instruction – using current student knowledge levels as a springboard to future academic success.

- Prepare students for today's high-tech economy.

- Encourage accountability for results.

- Bridge the digital divide—ultimately on a global basis.

Broad goals have been established for the our 1-1 Computing Program, including:

- Enhance student learning and achievement in core academic subjects with an emphasis on developing the knowledge and skills requisite to the establishment of a 21st century workforce.

- Provide greater access to equal education opportunities through ubiquitous access to technology.

- Foster effective use of wireless technology through systematic professional development for teachers, administrators and staff.

- Empower parents and caregivers with the tools to become more involved in their child's education.

- Support innovative structural changes in schools and sharing of best practices through the creation of human networks among program participants

QWK2LRN: The Company

As for the QWK2LRN initiative itself, the group has embraced many innovative changes in a short period of time. The organization has new executive management, a new model for sales and marketing, a new brand and image, a positive IBM partnership in place, a set of supportive suppliers , a global vision, and most importantly, an ingrained belief that innovation is not only essential for the successful development and ongoing deployment of the technology, but in the business processes of the organization as well. There are plans to roll this concept out to other cities in North and South America, and the timing will be based, in part, on the results we achieve in Detroit.

I am pleased to remain in support of this exciting new initiative as the non-Executive Chairman helping to steer much of the direction in what I believe is the final frontier for PC technology in education, a legacy I am proud of.

It is also rewarding to see that the PCs that have sometimes become dormant and unused can be resurrected and given a second life that will transform the lives of many young people globally. IBM remains extremely generous in its corporate giving and heartfelt commitment. We are fortunate also to have the support of several major foundations and companies. Together, we will pragmatically innovate in education, and we believe we will make a difference. Let's let Rip Van Winkle nap for a few more short years. When he awakes, we believe he will see a very different education landscape.

BUY A SHARE OF THE FUTURE IN YOUR COMMUNITY

These certificates make great holiday, graduation and birthday gifts that can be personalized with the recipient's name. The cost of one S.H.A.R.E. or one square foot is $54.17. The personalized certificate is suitable for framing and will state the number of shares purchased and the amount of each share, as well as the recipient's name. The home that you participate in "building" will last for many years and will continue to grow in value.

Here is a sample SHARE certificate:

HABITAT FOR HUMANITY

THIS CERTIFIES THAT
YOUR NAME HERE
HAS INVESTED IN A HOME FOR A DESERVING FAMILY

1985-2005
TWENTY YEARS OF BUILDING FUTURES IN OUR
COMMUNITY ONE HOME AT A TIME

1200 SQUARE FOOT HOUSE @ $65,000 = $54.17 PER SQUARE FOOT
This certificate represents a tax deductible donation. It has no cash value.

YES, I WOULD LIKE TO HELP!

I support the work that Habitat for Humanity does and I want to be part of the excitement! As a donor, I will receive periodic updates on your construction activities but, more importantly, I know my gift will help a family in our community realize the dream of homeownership. **I would like to SHARE in your efforts against substandard housing in my community!** *(Please print below)*

PLEASE SEND ME _____ SHARES at $54.17 EACH = $ $_____

In Honor Of: _____

Occasion: (Circle One)   HOLIDAY   BIRTHDAY   ANNIVERSARY

          OTHER: _____

Address of Recipient: _____

Gift From: _____ *Donor Address:* _____

Donor Email: _____

I AM ENCLOSING A CHECK FOR $ $_____ PAYABLE TO HABITAT FOR HUMANITY <u>OR</u> PLEASE CHARGE MY VISA OR MASTERCARD *(CIRCLE ONE)*

Card Number _____ Expiration Date: _____

Name as it appears on Credit Card _____ Charge Amount $ _____

Signature _____

Billing Address _____

Telephone # Day _____ Eve _____

PLEASE NOTE: Your contribution is tax-deductible to the fullest extent allowed by law.
Habitat for Humanity • P.O. Box 1443 • Newport News, VA 23601 • 757-596-5553
www.HelpHabitatforHumanity.org

Printed in the USA
CPSIA information can be obtained
at www.ICGtesting.com
JSHW012015140824
68134JS00025B/2424